THE BENCHMARKS SOURCEBOOK

THREE DECADES OF RELATED RESEARCH

THE BENCHMARKS SOURCEBOOK

THREE DECADES OF RELATED RESEARCH

Jean Brittain Leslie
Michael John Peterson

Center for Creative Leadership
Greensboro, North Carolina

The Center for Creative Leadership (CCL®) is an international, nonprofit educational institution founded in 1970 to advance the understanding, practice, and development of leadership for the benefit of society worldwide. As a part of this mission, it publishes books and reports that aim to contribute to a general process of inquiry and understanding in which ideas related to leadership are raised, exchanged, and evaluated. The ideas presented in its publications are those of the author or authors.

The Center thanks you for supporting its work through the purchase of this volume. If you have comments, suggestions, or questions about any CCL Press publication, please contact the Manager, Publication Development, at the address given below.

Center for Creative Leadership
Post Office Box 26300
Greensboro, North Carolina 27438-6300
www.ccl.org

Center for Creative Leadership
www.ccl.org

CCL Stock No. 356
©2011 Center for Creative Leadership

Published by CCL Press
Sylvester Taylor, Director of Assessments, Tools, and Publications
Peter Scisco, Manager, Publication Development
Karen Lewis, Associate Editor

Library of Congress Cataloging-in-Publication Data

Leslie, Jean Brittain.
   The benchmarks sourcebook : three decades of related research / Jean Brittain Leslie, Michael John Peterson.
      p. cm.
   "CCL Stock No. 356."
   Includes bibliographical references.
   ISBN 978-1-60491-085-8
1. Management—Research. 2. Leadership—Research. 3. Executive ability—Research.
4. 360-degree feedback (Rating of employees)—Research. I. Peterson, Michael John.
II. Center for Creative Leadership. III. Title.
   HD30.4.L47 2011
   650.072—dc22

                                                                        2010048883

Table of Contents

Overview

Since its introduction by the Center for Creative Leadership (CCL) in 1987, Benchmarks®, a 360-degree assessment, has been used by approximately 16,000 organizations and over 200,000 managers. Data collected through the administration of Benchmarks has resulted in large comprehensive databases. These data have provided the basis for numerous studies. While we have attempted to be exhaustive in our search for published works, we acknowledge that there are probably more studies that have taken place than the ones reported here.

Target Audience and Purpose

The annotations on published research were written for anyone who is interested in the research leading to the development and refinement of Benchmarks, the interpretation of the assessment's results, or the relationship of Benchmarks to other psychological assessments. They may also be helpful to anyone looking for paper, thesis, or dissertation topics.

Writing an annotated bibliography typically helps the author(s) gain a good perspective on a topic — in this case, the assessment of leadership. By reading it, you'll start to see the underlying key leadership issues and philosophical beliefs leading to the development of Benchmarks and what researchers argue are key issues related to the use of 360-degree feedback for leadership development by decade. You'll then be able to develop your own point of view.

The annotations on published research are organized in a way that orients the reader to the accumulation of research over the years — by decade, date, and author. Each decade starts with an introduction of the general focus of the publications for that time frame. An alternative method for organizing the research was to cluster it according to topic. For a list of annotations organized by topic, see appendix A.

Looking Forward

CCL maintains a number of databases on individuals who have participated in our programs or who have used our products. We encourage researchers to use these data for research. Names of individuals and organizations are protected and not released. Appendix B of this bibliography lists the guidelines to obtaining access to CCL's databases. Researchers interested in obtaining access to any CCL program or product database should submit a proposal to CCL.

The First Decade: 1983–1992

The majority of the summaries in this decade describe the research foundations of Benchmarks. Benchmarks is based on the results of two main areas of CCL research. These studies are most commonly referred to as the Key Events (or Lessons of Experience) and Executive Derailment research. The Key Events research program focuses on how executives learn and grow over their careers. The technical report *Key Events in Executives' Lives* (Lindsey, Homes, & McCall, 1987) summarizes CCL's first Lessons of Experience research project, which led to the development of Benchmarks. Executive Derailment research, on the other hand, compares and contrasts executives who are successful to those who derail, to determine the kind of development needed to reach senior-level positions.

These research programs provide insights into the dynamics of management development, including the skills, values, and perspectives that managers need to develop, as well as the potential flaws that they need to avoid or overcome. These studies also serve to reinforce the notion that assessment of both strengths and weaknesses is an important step in the leadership development process.

As the Benchmarks database grew, the latter part of the decade saw the introduction of studies of self-other rater agreement and its relationship to predicting leadership effectiveness.

McCall, M. W., Jr., & Lombardo, M. M. (1983, February). What makes a top executive? *Psychology Today, 17*(2), 26–31.

Based on a qualitative study of 21 derailed executives (those whose careers were stalled, plateaued, or over at the time of the interview) and 20 arriver executives (those who had reached their expected potential or were still expected to), McCall and Lombardo explored how and why executives were derailed in several Fortune 500 companies. The researchers interviewed human resource professionals and top executives, asking them to describe successful and derailed executives in their organizations.

Once the interviews were conducted, the qualitative analyses revealed 10 behavioral "fatal flaw" categories: insensitivity, arrogance, betrayal of trust, overly ambitious, performance problems, overmanaging, unable to staff effectively, unable to think strategically, unable to adapt to a boss with a different style, and overdependent on advocate or mentor. Further analyses suggested that situational changes of rising through the organizational hierarchy caused the derailment of executives. The authors found four basic situational causes for derailment: strengths became weaknesses, deficiencies eventually mattered, arrogance, and events conspired. Hence, both behavioral and situational factors led to derailment of executives.

However, both derailed and arriver executives made mistakes. These were found usually after the executives lost a compensating boss: entered a job for which they were not prepared, left a trail of small problems on their way up, were not scrutinized before arriving at the executive suite, and failed to be diplomatic once they entered the executive suite. Though not many mistakes were made, both groups took similar missteps.

When comparing derailed and arriver executives, the McCall and Lombardo study shows several interesting findings. First, the derailed group typically had a series of successes in a single function, whereas the arrivers achieved success in a variety of arenas, implying that a wealth of experiences is important to becoming an arriver. While both groups were problem solvers, the arrivers had a diversity of mentors. The derailed typically had a single mentor, which again suggests that the arrivers had a variety of contacts and experiences with which to solve problems. The qualitative analyses also suggested that how the executives handled adversity made a difference. The arrivers were found to be composed, confident, and articulate, whereas derailed executives were characterized as irritable under pressure and defensive over failures. The arrivers were also able to get along with all types of people. Therefore, while there is no fail-safe way of becoming an arriver, the McCall and Lombardo research suggests three critical components: diversity of contacts and experiences, getting along with all types of people, and handling adversity with poise and grace.

∗ ∗ ∗

McCall, M. W., Jr., & Lombardo, M. M. (1983). *Off the track: Why and how successful executives get derailed*. Greensboro, NC: Center for Creative Leadership.

This technical report echoes the previous McCall and Lombardo (1983) *Psychology Today* article. The authors' findings suggest that those who arrived and those who derailed were similar in many ways: they all were incredibly bright, were identified early, had outstanding track records, had few flaws, were ambitious, and had made many sacrifices. However, those who arrived had several additional qualities: they had diversity in their track records (that is, they had done several different things well), they maintained composure under stress, they handled mistakes with poise and grace, and they focused on problems and solved them. They also got along with all kinds of people, while remaining outspoken but not offensive. While both groups had several core attributes and few flaws, the research suggested that arrivers were more adaptive and sensitive to others.

✳ ✳ ✳

Lindsey, E., Homes, V., & McCall, M. W., Jr. (1987). *Key events in executives' lives* **(Report No. 32). Greensboro, NC: Center for Creative Leadership.**

This technical report deals primarily with exploring how life events or episodes affect the development of executives. Of the 191 executives considered for this qualitative study, interviews with 86 (usable $n = 79$) executives were purposively selected from three corporations. From the initial findings, three subsequent studies ($n = 112$) were conducted. The results suggested 31 original lesson categories and 16 event categories which were independently and inductively derived from the interview data. All events and lessons were assigned to a single category by trained coders, and disagreements were resolved by small-group consensus. Overall rater agreement was approximately 75 percent. Although chi-squared analyses were conducted, the primary statistic was percentage of individuals stating that they learned from a specific event.

Part 1 results focused on life events. These results suggest four key event categories: developmental assignments, hardships, other people, and other significant events. These key event categories were further subdivided. The developmental assignments category has five subcategories: starting from scratch, fix-it, project or task force, change in scope, and line-to-staff switch. The hardships category also has five subcategories: business failures and mistakes; demotions, missed promotions, or lousy jobs; breaking a rut; subordinate performance problems; and personal trauma. The other people category has two subcategories: role models and values playing out. The other significant events category has four subcategories: coursework, early work, first supervision, and purely personal.

Part 2 results focused on lessons learned. Splitting this part into two sections, the first section provides detailed information on 34 lessons, including their definitions, subtypes, and sources. The lessons were then ranked by how frequently they were mentioned. This section also makes suggestions regarding where a specific lesson might be learned. The second section organizes the 34 lessons according to five theoretical constellations: setting and implementing agendas, handling relationships, basic values, executive temperament, and personal awareness. This section also suggests how particular lessons relate to one another and to the executive job, which may prove useful in diagnosing managerial deficiencies and addressing them.

✳ ✳ ✳

Morrison, A. M., White, R. P., & Van Velsor, E. (1987). *Breaking the glass ceiling: Can women reach the top of America's largest corporations?* **Reading, MA: Addison-Wesley.**

Based on qualitative interviews with 76 women executives, this research documented the pressures these women felt being pioneers in their field. In general, this study found that women felt that they needed to be achievement-driven in the office, while still taking the major responsibility for the household and children. These women executives found switching between roles—being efficient and tough in the office, but tender and caring at home—to be extremely stressful. Female executives felt the additional pressure not to fail because doing so could possibly ruin the chances of success for other women.

While exploring the problems of female executives, the authors were also able to compare their analyses to former studies with men. The causes for derailment for both genders were very similar, yet there were also significant differences. Women had issues with image, while men had issues with developing relationships. The authors also suggest that women are expected to have more strengths and fewer faults than their male counterparts.

Since derailment was a common problem for males and females, the authors went on to give helpful suggestions on the importance of mentors, support systems, and asking for feedback. Furthermore, the authors suggest that credibility, strong advocacy, and pure luck are essential for women to break the glass ceiling.

The results were startling. After battling the corporate system, 25 percent of the women left corporate life to run their own companies, seek political office, or obtain a Ph.D. Moreover, with only 16 percent aspiring to the top executive level, the results suggest that most of these women did not desire to reach the top executive level. The authors conclude that the results suggest a clear waste of talent, which they speculated would continue in the United States for the next 20 years.

✳ ✳ ✳

Lombardo, M., & McCauley, C. (1988). *The dynamics of management derailment.* Greensboro, NC: Center for Creative Leadership.

Expanding upon the McCall and Lombardo (1983) qualitative derailment study, this study quantified derailment factors. After confirming low factor loadings of .4 for the 14 strength scales, Lombardo and McCauley clustered McCall and Lombardo's derailment characteristics. From this analysis, six flaw scales were derived: problems with interpersonal relationships, difficulty molding staff, difficulty making strategic transitions, lack of follow-through, overdependence on existing strengths, and strategic differences with management. These six flaw scales were then analyzed and compared to the Benchmarks skills and perspectives section.

Lombardo and McCauley first analyzed the reliability of the six flaw scales. The authors found that the average reliability was .85 for the six flaw scales, with a low of .7 for the overdependence on existing strengths scale and a high of .94 for the problems with interpersonal relationships scale. Next, the reliability of each of the six flaw scales was compared with that of the other five. The reliability was found to be an average of .48, with a low of .27 and a high of .75. Then the six flaw scales were correlated with the Benchmarks strength scales and were found to be either insignificant or negatively correlated with the strength scales. Hence, the six flaw scales are reliable, unique measures of their underlying constructs.

The results also suggest that the flaw scales capture 48 percent of the total derailment variance. Three scales—difficulty making strategic transitions, difficulty molding staff, and lack of follow-through—were found to have correlations ranging from .33 to .36, and each accounted for 13 percent of the derailment variance. Problems with interpersonal relationships and overdependence on existing strengths each accounted for 4 percent of the variance, and strategic differences with management accounted for only 1 percent of the variance. Hence, while no one derailment flaw appears to be critical, a combination of not following through on tasks, not being able to mold a staff, and having difficulty making transitions leads to 39 percent of the total derailment variance.

Using these scales, Lombardo and McCauley also discovered five key findings. First, while all of the flaws significantly correlated with future derailment, the strengths differed from a small .1 to a moderate .36 association. Second, the flaws varied widely across companies ($n = 8$) as to whether a particular flaw was more harmful to a manager's career than others. Third, based upon correlations between strengths and flaws, the authors found that participants scoring high on problems with interpersonal relationships, difficulty molding staff, difficulty making strategic transitions, and lack of follow-through were also viewed as low on straightforwardness, leading subordinates, and resourcefulness. Fourth, while all flaws were detrimental to job performance, the derailment flaws were found more critical to handling more challenging jobs. Finally, from a small sample of bosses ($n = 29$), with approximately half of the sample from one company, the authors were able to conclude that the scales were predictive of future derailment. In summary, the researchers both validated the derailment scales and found significant derailment results across the sample companies.

✳✳✳

Lombardo, M., Ruderman, M., & McCauley, C. (1988). Explanations of success and derailment in upper-level management positions. *Journal of Business and Psychology, 2,* **199–216.**

This study quantitatively compared successful ($n = 86$) and derailed ($n = 83$) managers, based on eight dimensions derived from several qualitative studies: handling business complexity, motivating and developing subordinates, honor, drive for excellence, organizational savvy, composure, sensitivity, and staffing. Using factors of both success and derailment, the results suggest significant differences among executives in three critical areas: managerial skills, personality factors, and the leadership of others. Derailed managers' skills were found to be lacking in the cognitive capacity to handle complex business ventures. They were also found to be lacking drive, abrasive, or deemed untrustworthy as compared to successful executives. In terms of leadership skills, derailed managers were found to be less able to direct, develop, and motivate subordinates. This investigation provided empirical evidence validating previous qualitative studies, demonstrated the importance of including factors of derailment, and provided a clearer understanding of the differences between successful and derailed executives.

✳✳✳

McCall, M. W., Jr., Lombardo, M. M., & Morrison, A. M. (1988). *The lessons of experience: How successful executives develop on the job.* **Lexington, MA: Lexington Books.**

Managers typically do not come into management positions possessing all of the knowledge, skills, and abilities necessary to advance. Managers must develop, and most development does not occur in the classroom, but from job assignments, other people such as bosses, and personal or professional hardships. This book, based on qualitative interviews with 191 accomplished and high-potential executives, describes key developmental events and the lessons that can be learned from them. The lessons are grouped into themes and represent fundamental executive skills and ways of thinking. The authors found five themes and their related lessons: setting and implementing agendas, handling relationships, basic values, executive temperament, and personal awareness. In 1990, Van Velsor and Hughes explored and elaborated upon these themes and their subsequent lessons with regard to gender differences.

✳ ✳ ✳

McCauley, C. D., Lombardo, M. M., & Usher, C. J. (1989). Diagnosing management development needs: An instrument based on how managers develop. *Journal of Management, 15*, 389–403.

McCauley, Lombardo, and Usher discuss the methods taken to develop Benchmarks, a 360-degree instrument designed to systematically assess managerial strengths and weaknesses. The instrument is unique in that it was developed from studying how managers learn, change, and grow, rather than from what they do. It also allows for a separate assessment of managerial flaws. Benchmarks was developed from content analysis of extensive interviews with executives, which resulted in 16 categories of critical developmental events and 34 categories of lessons learned from these events. Two hundred fifty-six items were drawn from the 34 categories of lessons learned and from the 10 categories of flaws responsible for derailment. These items were then given to 336 managers from eight Fortune 500 companies, who were rated by their immediate supervisors. From this sample, 108 items were sufficiently valid and reliable to keep, and they were then given to 75 managers who completed the items for themselves, and who were also rated by two or more coworkers. Section 1 Skills and Perspectives scale test-retest reliability coefficients for self-ratings ranged from $a = .62$ to $a = .87$ (mean $a = .72$). Test-retest coefficients for ratings by others were somewhat higher, ranging from $a = .71$ to $a = .95$ (mean $a = .85$). Section 2 Flaws scale test-retest reliability was lower for self (range $a = .47$ to $.63$; mean $a = .55$) and for others (range $a = .24$ to $.68$; mean $a = .43$). Validity tests were conducted on Benchmarks to assess whether the instrument demonstrated construct and criterion validity. When compared to ratings of promotability in hierarchy-based reward organizations, scales related to concern for others (such as building and mending relationships, $r = .38, p < .01$) and teamwork (such as team orientation, $r = .33, p < .01$) were more strongly associated with promotability than in performance-based reward organizations.

The research indicates that Benchmarks is both a reliable and valid tool for assessing managerial development in all types of organizations. Benchmarks offers unique information about managers, such as measures of straightforwardness, ability to balance opposites, balance of work and personal lives, personal styles that can lead to interpersonal problems, and overdependence, to the market-standard measures of performance. The conceptual difference between Benchmarks, which is solely based upon development and not performance, and its performance-based predecessors affords Benchmarks a unique and important place in managerial assessment.

∗ ∗ ∗

McCauley, C. D., & Lombardo, M. M. (1990). Benchmarks: An instrument for diagnosing managerial strengths and weaknesses. In K. Clark & M. Clark (Eds.), *Measures of leadership* (pp. 535–545). West Orange, NJ: Leadership Library of America.

Benchmarks was constructed based on several studies of executive growth to measure how managers develop. This 360-degree instrument consists of two sections: Section 1, composed of 16 subscales, is related to positive manager growth; and Section 2, composed of 6 subscales, is related to attributes that cause derailment. For Section 1, the indices of scale reliability were high for all subscales: average alpha = .88, average test-retest for self-ratings = .72, average test-retest for other ratings = .85, and average interrater reliability = .58. For Section 2, the indices of scale reliability were high for all subscales: average alpha = .83, average test-retest for self-ratings = .55, average test-retest for other ratings = .72, and average interrater reliability = .43. Therefore, Section 1 has high reliability, and Section 2 has acceptable reliability.

Benchmarks was used to assess managers across several areas—managerial success, organizational differences, and personal qualities—as well as against other feedback instruments. The Benchmarks ratings are significantly correlated with scales of managerial success such as performance evaluations ($n = 69$), boss's assessment of promotability ($n = 336$), independent criterion of promotability ($n = 64$), and whether the participant failed, did not change, or was promoted within 24 to 30 months of the Benchmarks ratings. The most predictive scales from Section 1 were those that clustered under adaptability, closely followed by hiring talented staff and creating a developmental work climate. The Benchmarks ratings also suggest differences between clannish and market-driven organizations, with market-driven organizations being significantly higher on decisiveness, hiring talent, and making strategic transitions, and clannish organizations being significantly higher on straight-forwardness and composure. Personal qualities were assessed by comparing the average ratings on Benchmarks by subordinates, peers, and superiors ($n = 111$) with participants' scores on the Myers-Briggs Type Indicator (MBTI), the Kirton Adaption-Innovation Inventory (KAI), and the Shipley Institute of Living Scale. On the Myers-Briggs, successful managers scored in the thinking direction, whereas derailment was more associated with the feeling direction. With regard to the KAI, successful promotion was more associated with innovation. Yet innovation was also positively linked to the derailment scales—problems with interpersonal relations and lack of follow-through.

Finally, Benchmarks was compared with the Management Skills Profile and the Management Practices Survey. All three measures target significant core concepts such as dealing with subordinates. However, the Benchmarks ratings also attempt to capture straightforwardness, how quickly a manager masters new knowledge, life-work balance, hiring talent, and confronting problem subordinates. Hence, Benchmarks provides a valid measure of managerial strengths and weaknesses that predict managerial success.

✽ ✽ ✽

Van Velsor, E., & Hughes, M. (1990). *Gender differences in the develop-ment of managers: How women managers learn from experience.* **Greensboro, NC: Center for Creative Leadership.**

Expanding upon the McCall et al. (1988) study of executive development, this qualitative study explored gender differences in the development of managers ($n = 267$). The samples were similar in most respects. The mean ages of this study were comparable, with the women averaging 41 years and the men 43 years. Both groups consisted of high-potential executives who were successful and demonstrated promise for future potential. Typically, the women held positions from director to senior vice president, as compared to the men, who held positions from general manager to chief executive. The men were from Fortune 50 companies, and the women were from Fortune 100 companies.

This study identified three critical learning arenas: assignments, hard-ships, and other people. For both men and women, most development came from their job assignments. Comparatively, men reported that 60 percent of their learning came from job assignments, and women reported 43 percent. Other people constituted 28 percent of learning for women, as compared with 14 percent for men. Finally, hardships were responsible for 22 percent of learning for women and 16 percent for men.

This study also found several common lessons for both men and women, regarding social interactions. These factors were directing and motivating employees, self-confidence, basic management values, how to work with executives, understanding other people's perspectives, dealing with people over whom you have no authority, and handling political situations. While all managers learned most lessons, there are several lessons unique to each gender. Additional lessons unique to the men ($n = 189$) involved learning about the business, technical/professional skills, coping with ambiguous situations, shouldering full responsibility, and persevering through adversity. The women ($n = 78$) learned more personal lessons, such as knowing personal limits and blind spots, taking charge of career, recognizing and seizing opportunities, coping with situations beyond their control, and knowing what interests them.

While this study's findings suggest that both men and women learn most from job assignments, women tend to learn a substantial amount from others as well. In general, women's lessons involved how to handle social and political situations. This study also suggests unique lessons to each gender: women learned more personal lessons, and men learned more about coping with and shouldering responsibility. Although there is large overlap between the lessons learned and arenas involved, women and men learn distinct lessons as well.

The Second Decade: 1993–2002

The second decade for Benchmarks research and publications was prolific. For the first time we see Benchmarks being used in doctoral dissertations (four annotations). This is our first indication that Benchmarks is becoming known to the academic community as a research tool. During this time frame, Benchmarks is also being recognized as a useful instrument by professionals through the Buros Mental Measurement Yearbook.

Key Events (or Lessons of Experience) studies remain popular (three annotations). However, the research samples broaden to include gender differences and country-specific samples (Japan and the Netherlands). Executive derailment studies also include cultural differences and non-U.S.-specific research samples (United States, Europe).

Publications during this decade explore the relationship between Benchmarks and personality measures (six annotations), the psychometric properties of Benchmarks (four annotations), and the influence of culture on the scores (two annotations). Other research topics for this decade include studies of self-other agreement (three annotations), leadership and derailment's relationship to emotional intelligence (one annotation), studies addressing 360-degree feedback and rating differences (two annotations), and studies addressing 360-degree feedback, goals, and change (one annotation).

Van Velsor, E., Taylor, S., & Leslie, J. B. (1993). An examination of the relationships among self-perception accuracy, self-awareness, gender, and leader effectiveness. *Human Resource Management, 32(2–3), 249–263.*

In this study, Van Velsor, Taylor, and Leslie focus on how self-other agreement on 360-degree feedback ratings is related to self-other ratings of self-awareness and leadership effectiveness, as well as examining gender differences in the likelihood of rater agreement and perceived self-awareness. Additionally, the article examines self-other agreement and gender differences in terms of knowledge of self and leader effectiveness.

Previous research has stressed that underlying assumptions of behavioral feedback ratings are based on two common assumptions: (1) that awareness of any discrepancy between how we see ourselves and how others see us will increase self-awareness and (2) that enhanced self-awareness is essential to maximum performance as a leader. In this study, data were collected from 648 randomly selected managers in the Center for Creative Leadership database, 168 upper-level managers from a Fortune 100 organization, and 79 hospital administrators, all of whom completed Benchmarks. Managers were placed into one of three categories: overraters (> 0.5 standard deviations), accurate raters (< +/- 0.5 standard deviations), and underraters (< -0.5 standard deviations), based on the average discrepancy between self-ratings and mean subordinate ratings across 15 of 16 Benchmarks scales.

Previous research suggested that women are more likely to underrate themselves on essential performance measures, but this study did not support gender differences between men and women. Across the three agreement groups, men and women did not vary significantly ($\chi^2 = 1.08$, $p = .58$), and discrepancy resulted from differences in both self-ratings and other ratings. Underraters consistently rated themselves lower than others and were consistently rated highest by their subordinates, and vice versa. Thus, underraters are perceived as more highly effective than either overraters or accurate raters. Although no gender differences were evident in terms of self-ratings, direct reports rated women as being significantly more self-aware than men ($t = 3.63$, $p < .02$). Surprisingly, underraters were rated as being more highly self-aware than either of the other two groups ($t = 3.87$, $t = 3.79$, $p < .01$).

The study lends new perspective to the growing role of women in organizations, and on their levels of effectiveness and self-awareness. These findings suggest that self-other discrepancy may not be measuring self-awareness, as conceptually thought, among underraters. The authors conclude that personality, statistical factors, and performance-related factors all play a role in ratings, and human resource managers should give credence to the magnitude and direction of discrepancies between self- and other ratings, until a logical interpretation of underraters can be reached.

Van Velsor, E., & Leslie, J. B. (1995). Why executives derail: Perspectives across time and cultures. *Academy of Management Executive*, *9*(4), 62–72.

Since the early executive derailment studies of the 1970s, several developmental insights have been provided to aspiring senior executives. This study investigated whether the derailment factors of early investigations have stood the test of time and whether these factors are valid across cultures. The results suggest four enduring themes: problems with interpersonal relationships, failure to meet business objectives, inability to build and lead a team, and inability to develop and adapt. One theme that has disappeared is overdependence on an advocate or mentor. However, a new theme has emerged: narrow business experience or limited functional orientation. Hence, the derailment perspective is informative and enduring.

With regard to cultural differences, two-thirds of European derailment was related to problems with interpersonal relations, as compared with one-third of American derailment. The inability to build and lead a team was related to 25 percent of European and 20 percent of American derailment. Two-thirds of both European and American derailment was related to the inability to change and adapt. Thus, the derailment factors are cross-cultural. The authors suggest that derailment is a developmental issue and not a values issue, indicating that managers can prevent derailment by working on the four derailment factors mentioned previously. However, managers must learn to understand the bases for their particular derailment factor or factors, and must resolve to work through the issues.

✳ ✳ ✳

Zedeck, S. (1995). Review of Benchmarks. In J. Conoley & J. Impara (Eds.), *The twelfth mental measurements yearbook* (Vol. 1, pp. 128–129). Lincoln, NE: Buros Institute of Mental Measurements.

The reviewer finds that overall, Benchmarks is a useful instrument to gather information about management style. The reviewer also positively notes that the Benchmarks process has all the ingredients for success: the instrument's research foundations are impressive, it yields impressive reliability data, the materials supporting the use and interpretation of the instrument are complete, and the norm base is sizable.

Zedeck criticizes the instrument for overrepresentation of white males during initial development. He further notes that females and racial and ethnic minorities are underrepresented in the 1992 norm group. Finally, the reviewer calls into question the long-term usefulness of the Benchmarks feedback process on workplace development, learning, and success.

✳ ✳ ✳

Fleenor, J. W., McCauley, C. D., & Brutus, S. (1996). Self-other rating agreement and leader effectiveness. *Leadership Quarterly*, 7, 487–506.

Fleenor, McCauley, and Brutus examine two models of self-other agreement of 360-degree feedback ratings in predicting leader effectiveness. Using differences between standardized mean self- and subordinate ratings of performance on the Benchmarks instrument, 2,056 managers were divided into a model with four categories: overestimators (self-scores > 0.5 standard deviations from the mean subordinate rating); underestimators (self-scores < -0.5 standard deviations from the mean subordinate rating); in agreement–good (self-scores within +/-0.5 standard deviations from the mean, and average subordinate rating above the sample mean); and in agreement–poor (self-scores within +/-0.5 standard deviations from the mean, and average subordinate rating below the sample mean). Next, managers were further subdivided into a six-factor model with two more categories: overestimators–good (self-scores < -0.5 standard deviations from the mean subordinate rating, and average subordinate rating above the sample mean) and underestimators–poor (self-scores < -0.5 standard deviations from the mean subordinate rating, and average subordinate rating below the sample mean). These differences were then compared to boss/superior ratings of effectiveness for the manager. With the four-category model and using Tukey's comparison test, supervisors appeared to rate in agreement–good raters (range of means = 3.50–4.24) and underestimators (range of means = 3.40–4.16) as more effective on all scales than overestimators (range of means = 3.29–4.03). Using the six-category model, in agreement–good raters (range of means = 3.51–4.24) were not seen as significantly more effective than overestimators–good raters (range of means = 3.75–4.22). Results indicated that differences in effectiveness between underestimators, overestimators, and in-agreement raters appear to be the result of differences in others' (subordinate/supervisor) ratings, not the result of self-other rating discrepancies per se. These differences went away when performance was statistically controlled for. Therefore, it is imperative to examine the six-category model to avoid such effects of rating bias as leniency and rating inflation.

✳ ✳ ✳

Hood, S. J. (1996). A study of self and direct report perceptions of the skills and performance competencies important for superintendent effectiveness. *Dissertation Abstracts International: Section A. Humanities and Social Sciences, 57(5-A), 1928.*

Hood's dissertation uses CCL's 1995 Leadership Development Program archival data of 59 Ohio public school superintendents and their direct reports to determine superintendent effectiveness as perceived by direct reports and superintendents. Hood employed two surveys to determine superintendent effectiveness: Benchmarks and a superintendent effectiveness questionnaire based on the eight professional standards established in 1993 by the American Association of School Administrators.

Hood mailed her superintendent effectiveness questionnaire to superintendents who agreed to participate in the effectiveness research. The superintendents were instructed to self-report on their effectiveness and to have the same five direct reports who completed Benchmarks also complete the questionnaire. A useable 47 superintendent questionnaires and 224 matching direct report responses were received.

Results of exploratory and confirmatory factor analyses reveal measurement models which indicate that superintendents and their direct reports view leadership and effectiveness as two major constructs. Results of structural equation models indicate that there is no relationship between these leadership skills and the effectiveness measures.

✳ ✳ ✳

Leslie, J. B., & Van Velsor, E. (1996). *A look at derailment today: North America and Europe* (Report No. 169). Greensboro, NC: Center for Creative Leadership.

This technical report is similar to the article the authors published in the *Academy of Management Executive* journal (Van Velsor & Leslie, 1995).

✳ ✳ ✳

Center for Creative Leadership. (1997). CPI/MBTI/Benchmarks study. In *Benchmarks: A manual and trainer's guide*. Greensboro, NC: Center for Creative Leadership.

In 1993, J. W. Fleenor and E. Van Velsor completed an archival database study of the relationship between Benchmarks and rated behavior in a CCL program (Energy International and Earth II), and between Benchmarks ratings by other superiors, peers, and direct reports and two personality measures, the Myers-Briggs Type Indicator (MBTI) ($n = 788$) and the California Psychological Inventory (CPI) ($n = 235$). Correlations of the behavioral assessment and Benchmarks revealed several results. On the Benchmarks scale, doing whatever it takes was significantly related to ratings of leading the discussion and influencing others during the behavioral assessment (Energy International). Motivating others was related to being a quick study and negatively related to balance between personal life and work. Verbal effectiveness was related to resourcefulness, doing whatever it takes, and being a quick study, and negatively related to balance between personal life and work. Activity level, leading the discussion, influencing, problem analysis, and task orientation were also negatively related to balance between personal life and work. Pearson correlations between the MBTI scale feeling and eight Benchmarks scales—leading employees, setting a developmental climate, work team orientation, hiring talented staff, compassion and sensitivity, self-awareness, putting people at ease, and acting with flexibility—were found among direct report ratings. The relationships between the MBTI scales with average peer ratings from Benchmarks were as follows: Feeling was positively related to four Benchmarks scales—setting a developmental climate, compassion and sensitivity, self-awareness, and putting people at ease. Thinking was negatively correlated with problems with interpersonal relationships, and extraversion was related to putting people at ease. Benchmarks ratings by other superiors were correlated with MBTI scales as follows: Extraversion and feeling were related to putting people at ease. The correlations of the CPI scales with average direct report ratings from Benchmarks were as follows: Self-control, achievement via conformance, and internality were negatively correlated with lack of follow-through. Internality also was negatively related to overdependence. The correlations of the CPI scales with average peer ratings from Benchmarks are as follows: Dominance was correlated with doing what-ever it takes. Well-being was negatively related to difficulty in molding a staff. Achievement via independence and psychological-mindedness were correlated with being a quick study. Femininity/masculinity was negatively related to resourcefulness, doing whatever it takes, being a quick study, leading direct reports, setting a developmental climate, confronting problem employees, and acting with flexibility. Femininity/masculinity was positively correlated with difficulty in molding a staff and difficulty in making strategic transitions. Empathy was positively related to doing whatever it takes, leading employees, setting a developmental climate, and acting with flexibility. Empathy was negatively correlated with difficulty in making strategic transitions. Internality was negatively related to decisiveness. The correlations of the CPI scales with Benchmarks ratings by other superiors are as follows: Sociability was negatively correlated with straightforwardness and composure. Socialization was negatively related to balance between personal life and work, and positively related to putting people at ease. Achievement via independence was correlated with resourcefulness and being a quick study. Intellectual efficiency was related to decisiveness. Independence was negatively correlated with compassion and sensitivity. Norm-favoring was related to balance between personal life and work, lack of follow-through, and strategic differences with management. Internality was negatively correlated with lack of follow-through.

＊＊＊

Center for Creative Leadership. (1997). Gender differences: Updates on Key Events research for women of the 90's. In *Benchmarks: A manual and trainer's guide*. Greensboro, NC: Center for Creative Leadership.

Researchers at the Center for Creative Leadership conducted a reexamination of Key Events for women. The sample included 145 women who attended the Center's Executive Women Workshop from May 1991 through January 1993. They responded to the Key Events question used in the Lessons of Experience and Glass Ceiling research.

The first research question asked whether the mix of learning sources had shifted so that women were learning more from job assignments than they had previously. This shift had occurred. The learning from assignments increased slightly, and the learning from other people decreased substantially. Learning from hardship events increased slightly, putting the proportion of learnings that are from hardships 6 percent higher for women in the early 1990s than for women a decade before. Learning from other events remained approximately the same between men and women and from one decade to the next, but coursework learning dropped. The second question asked whether women currently in the workplace reported a different mix of assignments than women did in the original studies, and it could be answered in the affirmative. Women in this study reported three times as many fix-it assignments (proportionally) than the women in the Glass Ceiling study, and they reported a proportion of starting-from-scratch assignments similar to the men in Lessons of Experience. Key events for women that were changes in scope dropped dramatically. Project/task force and line-to-staff switches remained approximately the same. In comparison to the men's findings, women studied did not report having the same variety and intensity of job assignments as men did; specifically, they lacked experiences with starting-from-scratch and fix-it assignments. Also, women reported more learning from significant relationships and less learning from job assignments than men did.

＊＊＊

Center for Creative Leadership. (1997). Gender differences: Validity study. In *Benchmarks: A manual and trainer's guide*. Greensboro, NC: Center for Creative Leadership.

This study of hospital administrators compares the validity of Benchmarks for males and for females. Benchmarks scores and criterion measures were available for 53 female and 26 male administrators. Criterion measures consisted of overall ratings of the managers' performance, promotability, and derailment potential. These ratings were provided by the same coworkers who completed Benchmarks on the individual. Direct report raters also indicated the degree to which they were satisfied with the manager as a leader. The male and female samples were comparable in terms of age and organizational level. All of the Benchmarks scales were correlated significantly with at least one of four criterion measures. When comparing the correlations in the women's sample with those in the men's sample, few significant differences were found (8 out of 88 comparisons). Correlations were higher in the men's sample between decisiveness and derailment potential, and between confronting problem employees and both promotability and satisfaction. Correlations were stronger in the women's sample between strategic differences with management and both promotability and performance, between putting people at ease and satisfaction, between straightforwardness and composure and satisfaction, and between problems with interpersonal relationships and satisfaction.

∗ ∗ ∗

Center for Creative Leadership. (1997). Organizational cultural differences. In *Benchmarks: A manual and trainer's guide*. Greensboro, NC: Center for Creative Leadership.

Using the Benchmarks database, this study compares scores of managers from different organizational cultures and examines whether particular scales would be more predictive of success than others. Three organizations in the database were classified as hierarchy based and three as performance based. The degree to which managers in the two types of organizations were seen by their bosses as possessing the 16 managerial skills and perspectives in Section 1 of Benchmarks and the six problem areas in Section 2 were examined. In addition, relationships between these characteristics and the bosses' assessments of the managers' promotability were also explored in the two types of organizations. Significant mean score differences between managers in hierarchy-based organizations and performance-based organizations occurred only on the decisiveness scale ($t = -2.73, p < .01$). In other words, culture did not seem to have much impact on how a manager was rated by his or her boss. However, there were significant differences between the types of organizations on the correlations between scale scores and bosses' overall ratings of promotability. In other words, some skills, perspectives, or flaws were seen as more related to continued success in one type of organization than in the other type. Of the management skills and perspectives scales, resourcefulness ($z = -2.09, p < .05$) and doing whatever it takes ($z = -1.90, p < .05$) were strongly related to ratings of promotability in both groups with somewhat stronger correlations in the performance-based organizations. Building and mending relationships ($r = .42$), compassion and sensitivity ($r = .25$), team orientation ($r = .39$), and self-awareness ($r = .50$) were more strongly related to ratings of promotability in the hierarchy-based organizations, while being a quick study ($r = .62$), decisiveness ($r = .35$), and hiring talented staff ($r = .55$) were more strongly related to promotability in the performance-based organizations. On the problem area scales, stronger negative relationships were found for difficulty in molding a staff ($r = -.60$) and in making strategic transitions ($r = -.58$) in the performance-based organizations. Problems with interpersonal relationships ($r = -.30$) were more negatively related to ratings of promotability in the hierarchy-based organizations. An important implication of this analysis is that what is most important for success in one organization might not be as important in another organization. This led to the addition of a section to Benchmarks that allows the individuals who are rating a manager to also give that manager some input on what characteristics they see as most important for success in that particular organization.

✳ ✳ ✳

Center for Creative Leadership. (1997). Race differences: Are African-American managers rated differently than white managers? In *Benchmarks: A manual and trainer's guide*. Greensboro, NC: Center for Creative Leadership.

J. W. Fleenor investigates whether African American managers, as a group, are rated differently on Benchmarks than white managers. Two groups of CCL participants who had received Benchmarks feedback participated in the study. The first group consisted of 130 African American middle-level managers from the business sector. A similar group of 130 white managers was chosen to participate. There were 67 males and 63 females in each of the groups, which were almost identical on other demographic variables such as age and education level. The researcher conducted a statistical analysis to determine whether there were significant differences between the two groups on Benchmarks. He found that direct reports rated the African American managers significantly higher on 12 of the 16 Benchmarks scales, and peers rated them higher on 9 of the scales. All raters gave African American managers higher ratings on work team orientation. There were no differences on boss ratings between African American and white managers on the other scales. Bosses and peers rated white managers significantly higher on being a quick study and on decisiveness.

$$* * *$$

Center for Creative Leadership. (1997). Relationships with other psychological instruments. In *Benchmarks: A manual and trainer's guide*. Greensboro, NC: Center for Creative Leadership.

This research looks at how ratings by others on Benchmarks are related to scores on several self-report psychological instruments. Average ratings on Benchmarks by coworkers (direct reports, peers, and superiors) for 111 managers were correlated with scores on the Myers-Briggs Type Indicator (MBTI), the Kirton Adaption-Innovation Inventory (KAI), and the Shipley Institute of Living Scale. Results showed the extraversion-introversion, thinking-feeling, and adaptive-innovative dimensions were associated more with coworkers' perceptions of a manager's skills and perspectives. The sensing-intuition, judging-perceiving, and Shipley scores were fairly independent of coworkers' perceptions. The more extraverted managers were seen as more decisive ($r = -.30, p = <.01$) and more compassionate and sensitive ($r = -.18, p = <.10$). They are also rated as better at hiring talented staff ($r = -.18, p = <.10$), building and mending relationships ($r = -.19, p = <.05$), and putting people at ease ($r = -.35, p = <.01$). Managers who focus more on feelings when making decisions are also seen by their coworkers as more compassionate and sensitive ($r = .25, p = <.01$) and better able to build and mend relationships ($r = .24, p = <.01$) and put people at ease ($r = .31, p = <.01$). In addition, these managers are seen as being more self-aware ($r = .26, p = <.01$), acting with more flexibility ($r = .20, p = <.05$), having fewer interpersonal problems ($r = -.25, p = <.01$), and having better balance between their work and personal life ($r = .22, p = <.05$). However, managers who focus more on logical outcomes when making decisions are seen as better at confronting problem employees ($r = .08, p = <.10$). Both types of problem-solving styles as measured by the KAI are associated with particular managerial strengths and weaknesses. The more innovative managers are seen as more likely to be decisive ($r = .41$, $p = <.01$) and to take charge and persevere, doing whatever it takes ($r = .20$, $p = <.05$). However, they are also seen as having more interpersonal problems ($r = .24$, $p = <.01$) and as not always following through ($r = .16$, $p = <.10$). The more adaptive managers are seen as being more straightforward and composed ($r = -.17$, $p = <.10$) and better at building and mending relationships ($r = -.17$, $p = <.10$). None of the Benchmarks and Shipley scores were statistically significantly correlated.

✳✳✳

Fleenor, J. (1997). The relationship between the MBTI and measures of personality and performance in management groups. In C. Fitzgerald & L. K. Kirby (Eds.), *Developing leaders: Research and applications in psychological type and leadership development* (pp. 115–138). Palo Alto, CA: Davies-Black.

This chapter discusses the relationship between the Myers-Briggs Type Indicator (MBTI), measures of personality, and performance in management groups. The sample comprised 26,477 mostly middle- and upper-level managers who attended CCL programs from 1985 to 1993. The mean age was 41, with 17 years of education. In this chapter, relationships between the MBTI and several measures of personality and performance were discussed. The MBTI was related to two well-known personality measures, the California Psychological Inventory (CPI) and the Fundamental Interpersonal Relations Orientation-Behavior (FIRO-B), and was also correlated with the Kirton Adaption-Innovation Inventory (KAI), a measure of creativity and problem solving. Specifically, intuition and perceiving were correlated with higher innovative KAI scores. Coworker ratings from the Leadership Style Indicator (LSI) were found to be related to MBTI types. However, the MBTI did not strongly relate to two Leaderless Group Discussion (LGD) scales. Finally, using measures of occupational stress (Occupational Stress Inventory) and job satisfaction (Managerial Job Satisfaction Questionnaire), introverts appear to be more susceptible to occupational stress and experience less job satisfaction than extraverts.

✳✳✳

Van Velsor, E., & Fleenor, J. (1997). The MBTI and leadership skills: Relationships between the MBTI and four 360-degree management feedback instruments. In C. Fitzgerald & L. K. Kirby (Eds.), *Developing leaders: Research and applications in psychological type and leadership development* **(pp. 139–162). Palo Alto, CA: Davies-Black.**

This review discusses the relationships between MBTI preferences and four 360-degree management feedback instruments, and found that most managers rated themselves as either extravert or introvert, sensing, thinking, and judging. Van Velsor and Fleenor found that extraverts tend to see themselves as skilled in management and leadership. Managers with a preference for sensing, thinking, and judging are more likely to get favorable ratings from others on administrative or task management scales. Coworkers also tend to prefer administrators with a preference for feeling. Recognizing others' contributions, putting people at ease, and building relationships are less important to thinking managers. In general, the four studies demonstrate that MBTI preference is related to leadership strengths and developmental needs of managers.

✳✳✳

Wise, P. G. (1997). Rating differences in multi-rater feedback: A new look at an old issue. *Dissertation Abstracts International: Section B. Sciences and Engineering,* **58(6-B), 3352.**

Wise's dissertation uses CCL's 1996 Benchmarks archival data of 1,173 managers to examine rater group differences on each Benchmarks skill. Structural equation modeling (ABG-type analyses) was used to test for the presence of two particular types of rater group differences: (1) construct definition differences, and (2) rating scale point differences. Wise found the construct validity (factor structure) of 14 of the 16 scales was upheld across rater groups. Only two dimensions exhibited evidence of multidimensionality ("gamma" differences, in ABG terms) across groups. She concludes these results provide evidence that well-constructed scales can exhibit similar factor structure across different rater groups. Fourteen dimensions exhibited rating scale point definition differences ("beta" differences, in ABG terms). This finding is problematic because in multirater feedback efforts, each rater group should be defining rating scale points similarly in order to compare mean ratings across groups.

✳✳✳

Atwater, L., Ostroff, C., Yammarino, F., & Fleenor, J. (1998). Self-other agreement: Does it matter? *Personnel Psychology, 51*, 577–598.

In this paper, Atwater, Ostroff, Yammarino, and Fleenor examine agreement between self-other ratings in 360-degree feedback and the direct ramifications this agreement has on individual and organizational impact. Previous research was controversial because there was no consensus as to whether self-other agreement in 360-degree feedback would influence whether the self-rater was effective on the job. The study addressed methodological problems with previous research that had led to this controversy, such as the neglect of researchers to properly conceptually grasp what self-other agreement means and the improper operational definition of self-other agreement. Atwater et al. used both type or direction of agreement (over-, in, and underagreement), as well as the degree of agreement and level of behavior as rated by self and other, to consider whether the effects of self-other agreement on outcomes were being properly assessed. They proposed that self-ratings and other ratings should be viewed as separate measures and that the form of the relationship between self-ratings, other ratings, and outcomes be viewed in three dimensions. Data were collected from about 1,460 managers who participated in a leadership development program, using Benchmarks. Other ratings were aggregated for analysis, which was justified based on the intraclass correlation range that was computed from a previous comparable sample (.47 to .70). The outcome measure for this study was a 16-item scale of managerial effectiveness filled out by each manager's supervisor. Using regression analyses for self-ratings and subordinate ratings separately, the data indicate that self-rating predicts supervisor effectiveness ratings ($b = .36$, $p = .05$) and subordinate ratings predict supervisor effectiveness ratings ($b = .39$, $p = .04$). When aggregating the data, regression analyses demonstrate that the total variance accounted for by the model indicates that surface analysis is needed. Surface analyses indicate that (1) effectiveness ratings are very high when self-other ratings are in agreement and very high, (2) effectiveness decreases as self-other ratings agree and become lower, and (3) effectiveness ratings increase again slightly when self-other ratings agree and are very low.

Results of the study lend support for considering both self and other agreement to managerial outcomes of effectiveness and performance, although the relationship was found to be more complex than previously conceptualized. In addition, the study shows the importance of properly conceptualizing the form of the agreement relationship, and then appropriately testing the hypotheses.

* * *

Brutus, S., Fleenor, J. W., & London, M. (1998). Does 360-degree feedback work in different industries? A between-industry comparison of the reliability and validity of multi-source performance ratings. *Journal of Management Development, 17(5)*, 177–190.

Brutus, Fleenor, and London examine the interaction of self-other agreement ratings and organization type to predict performance evaluations. Previous research had examined the predictive validity of 360-degree feedback within one sample, generally one organization, but did not account for systematic differences between organizations within an industry or between industries. This systematic difference may impact how managers view the practice of using 360-degree feedback to make decisions, as to whether the process is reliable and valid within their industry. Conceivably, industries could vary on a number of dimensions that could affect multisource ratings. By examining self-other rating differences between six organization types (manufacturing, finance, education, health, government, and military), the study investigates variation on the outcome variables of leniency/ favorability, interrater agreement, and self-other agreement rating. Interrater and self-other agreement was measured using Benchmarks, and supervisor effectiveness was measured using the 16 items contained in the Benchmarks Handling Challenging Jobs section. The study also controls for variability within and across each organization type in terms of race, gender, age, education, and organization level (upper- to middle-level managers), which could skew results across organizations. Results indicate that (1) for all rating sources except supervisor, educational organization employees received the highest ratings (mean = 3.96), while those in manufacturing received the lowest (mean = 3.82); (2) most of the significant differences in ratings fell along the public/private sector dichotomy—those in the public sector (education, military, and government) were significantly higher than those in the private sector (manufacturing, finance, health); (3) although effect size was moderate, organization type has the most impact on peer rating ($n^2 = .06$), followed by supervisor and subordinate rating ($n^2 = .03$); and (4) organization type had the smallest effect size on self-ratings ($n^2 = .01$). Additionally, the level of interrater agreement was tested and was found to be higher in educational and manufacturing organizations than in the military [$F(10, 984) = 3.45, p < .01$]. Results indicate that there seemed to be small yet significant differences in rater agreement between organization type, with education and manufacturing generating fairly high agreement. In examining the relationship between effectiveness and performance ratings, there was (1) a high correlation between supervisor ratings and effectiveness

($r = .45$); (2) a moderate correlation between effectiveness and peer ratings
($r = .28$) and subordinate ratings ($r = .20$); and (3) a low correlation between
self-ratings and effectiveness ($r = .10$). Generally, these relationships were
highest for educational institutions and lowest for the military.

The study indicates that there are significant, albeit small, systematic
differences between organization types in the level of ratings, interrater
agreement, and the relationship between effectiveness and performance
ratings. The current findings suggest that researchers and practitioners
should not automatically assume that 360-degree feedback works the same
way in all organizations.

✳ ✳ ✳

Greguras, G. J., & Robie, C. (1998). A new look at within-source inter-rater reliability of 360-degree feedback ratings. *Journal of Applied Psychology, 83*(6), 960–968.

Using generalizability theory, this study is a more thorough examination of
within-source interrater reliability because it includes peer and subordinate
as well as supervisor responses on the Benchmarks instrument. It also
employs restricted maximum likelihood estimation (REML) to analyze
the data collected from 153 American managers, which is an improvement
over the expected means squares (EMS) method used in previous studies.
Results suggest little within-source agreement. Most of the error variance is
attributable to the combined rater main effect and Rater x Ratee interaction.
To reach acceptable levels of reliability, more subjects are required.
However, these findings suggest that supervisors are the most reliable raters,
followed by peers, then subordinates.

✳ ✳ ✳

Brutus, S., Fleenor, J. W., & McCauley, C. D. (1999). Demographic and personality predictors of congruence in multi-source ratings. *Journal of Management Development, 18*(5), 417–435.

Brutus, Fleenor, and McCauley examine specific demographic and
personality variables believed to exert an effect on multisource ratings. These
possible determinants of rating congruence were shown to predict the extent
to which self-ratings converge with the ratings of supervisors, subordinates,
and peers. Data were collected from 1,014 managers who participated in a
leadership development program, and included Benchmarks, demographic
questions (age, gender, ethnicity, and organization level), and the California

Psychological Inventory. Using regression analyses, it was shown that
(1) gender significantly predicted peer (b = .032) and subordinate ratings (b = .045) but not self-ratings—self-ratings of females are in line with their ratings by subordinates and peers, whereas males tend to overrate themselves;
(2) ethnicity predicted both self-ratings (b = .034) and others' ratings (b = .045 for peers, b = .035 for subordinates); (3) the discrepancy between self- and supervisor ratings increases with age—older workers are more likely to overrate than younger workers (b = .030); and (4) there were differences in the prediction of self-ratings and the prediction of subordinate and peer ratings by organization level—at low organization levels, managers tend to underestimate their performance in relation to subordinates and peers, whereas at higher levels managers tend to overestimate their performance in relation to subordinates and peers. Additionally, results indicate that personality variables influence self-ratings and others' ratings differently. Dominance, social presence, good impression, and communality predicted self-ratings and others' ratings differently, whereas well-being, social acceptance, empathy, and psychological-mindedness did not. Specifically, (1) empathy was the only significant predictor of ratings across all four sources; and (2) ethnicity significantly predicted the ratings from all but one source, supervisor ratings. The study was successful in identifying individual characteristics that account for self-other rating congruence, but acknowledges it would be beneficial to understand how these individual characteristics affect responsiveness to feedback.

✳ ✳ ✳

Brutus, S., London, M., & Martineau, J. (1999). The impact of 360-degree feedback on planning for career development. *Journal of Management Development*, 18(8), 676–693.

Brutus, London, and Martineau examine the relationship between 360-degree feedback to managers, as determined by Benchmarks, and subsequent selection of developmental goals, as measured by Reflections. Based on the assumption that feedback information will ultimately lead managers to alter their behavior to improve performance, the study hypothesized that performance ratings would be negatively related to setting developmental goals. Additionally, the hypotheses that supervisor ratings would have a greater impact on goal setting than peer or direct report ratings and that self-other discrepancies in feedback would be related to goal selection were tested. Data from 2,163 managers indicated that multisource feedback was directly related to developmental goal selection. Twelve of the 14 goal coefficients in the nine models tested were significant and negative (range of -.27 to -1.00; $p < .05$), indicating that lower ratings do indeed lead to developmental goal selection. Only two of the nine regression equations indicated that supervisor ratings led to developmental goal setting, as compared to eight of nine for subordinate ratings and four of nine for peer ratings. Results indicate that contrary to the hypothesis, peer and direct report ratings are predictive of subsequent goal selection. There was a logical connection between a majority of goals selected and the underlying performance dimension that best predicts them. By adding the interaction term of self x other to the regression equations testing rater feedback and goal selection, the hypothesis that self-other discrepancies would predict goal selection did not yield a log greater than -2, and was not supported. Therefore, direct feedback itself, rather than its relationship to self-perception, predicted goal selection. The study concluded that more research is needed to understand the degree to which self-evaluations influence the use of external evaluations for developmental planning, as well as the developmental process beyond goal setting.

❊ ❊ ❊

Raju, N. S., Leslie, J. B., McDonald-Mann, D., & Craig, B. (1999). Content validation. In *Benchmarks: A manual and trainer's guide*. Greensboro, NC: Center for Creative Leadership.

Items across the 21 scales of Benchmarks were examined for measurement equivalence using the Item Response Theory (IRT)-based DFIT framework. The IRT-DFIT framework, a type of statistical analysis for detecting differential item functioning (DIF), is one of the most important psychometric analyses in validating a test for use in two or more cultural or language populations. Racial (Caucasian American and African American) and translation comparisons were made (U.S. English, U.K. English, and French) to eliminate items that show bias or favoritism toward one group over another.

Five comparisons and samples were selected for this investigation. A U.S. random sample of 1,019 cases was drawn from the 1996 Benchmarks database. The U.S. Caucasian American sample was a subsample of the U.S. random sample. Data from the 1997 Benchmarks database were combined to generate the U.S. African American sample for a total of 588 cases. All available Benchmarks data were used to define the French and U.K. comparisons. In each of the five samples, only managers with boss, self-, direct report, and peer ratings were included. The boss rating source was designated as the reference group in all the comparisons.

The results of the DFIT analyses indicated a substantial or high degree of measurement equivalence for Caucasian Americans and African Americans. Only a total of four items with significant DIF were found. The comparison of the U.S. boss versus French boss had the highest number of items (39) with significant DIF. The U.S. boss versus U.K. boss comparison had no significant DIF items. Overall, the extent of measurement equivalence appears to be substantial for the Benchmarks survey.

Items that exhibited measurement nonequivalence or DIF were reviewed by subject matter experts to determine their cultural appropriateness or poor adaptation of the translation. Items that could not be revised were eliminated from Benchmarks.

✳✳✳

Conway, J. M. (2000). Managerial performance development constructs and personality correlates. *Human Performance*, *13*(1), 23–46.

Conway discusses the identification and underlying motivational determinants of managerial performance development correlates, as well as the examination of rater differences. California Personality Inventory (CPI), Myers-Briggs Type Indicator (MBTI), and Benchmarks data were collected from 2,110 managers from a variety of industries and management levels. Exploratory factor analysis of the 16 Benchmarks scales indicated the existence of five developmental constructs: (1) Interpersonal effectiveness roughly corresponds with highest loading scale putting people at ease (loading of .94); (2) Willingness to handle difficult situations roughly corresponds with half of the Benchmarks construct meeting job challenges, decisiveness (loading of .84); (3) Teamwork and personal adjustment highest loading factor was scale work team orientation (loading of .59); (4) Adaptability roughly corresponds with second half of the Benchmarks construct meeting job challenges, being a quick study (loading of .80); and (5) Leadership and development highest loading factor was setting a developmental climate (loading of .67). Results suggest that the underlying personality determinants of the managerial performance development correlates were as follows: (1) Interpersonal effectiveness correlated most highly with CPI empathy ($a = .26$) and tolerance ($a = .17$) and MBTI thinking-feeling ($a = .30$); (2) Willingness to handle difficult decisions showed significant high correlations with CPI dominance ($a = .34$), independence ($a = .30$), self-acceptance (a = .29), and social presence (a = .22); (3) Teamwork and personal adjustment demonstrated strong relationships with CPI socialization (a = .22) and self-control (a = .22); (4) Adaptability correlated most highly with CPI intellectual efficiency (a = .20) and achievement via independence (a = .22); and (5) Leadership and development was most strongly associated with CPI empathy (a = .23) and self-acceptance (a = .17) and MBTI thinking-feeling (a = .17). Rating sources (supervisor, peer, subordinate, and self) showed some differences in their responses, though no hypotheses were made to explain or address this variance. The author describes this paper as being a catalyst to further understanding what causes managers to manifest certain behaviors, as a factor of their underlying personality traits, which could be a useful tool in the selection process.

✱ ✱ ✱

Conway, R. L. (2000). The impact of coaching mid-level managers utilizing multi-rater feedback. *Dissertation Abstracts International: Section A. Humanities and Social Sciences, 60*(7-A), 2672.

Conway's dissertation measures improvement in the accuracy of participants' self-perceptions as a result of 360-degree feedback and coaching, compared to the perceptions of others. Subjects selected for this study were mid-level managers in a large state agency. Conway used two instruments in his research: Benchmarks and the Developmental Challenge Profile (DCP), an instrument designed to help participants understand the dynamics of their current assignment and to better identify learning strategies for increasing their leadership skills on the job. The participants in this study received their instrument results, along with three coaching sessions, designed to identify strengths and weaknesses and create an action plan.

With one exception, there were no significant differences found between the subjects in this study and a normative group of public sector managers. Also, no significant differences were found in time 1 and time 2 data to support that feedback and coaching significantly improved the accuracy of participants' self-perceptions or individual skills. Study subjects did perceive that feedback and coaching had a positive impact on their leadership skills.

Conway's research recommends that (1) the process of ongoing multi-rater feedback and coaching be expanded to a larger population, (2) the time frame for administering surveys be expanded to 18 months, (3) mid-level managers should formally include developmental goals in annual review processes, and (4) institutions should review group reports to identify needed skill development and to better target in-service training.

∗ ∗ ∗

Center for Creative Leadership. (2001). Japanese key events. In
**   *Benchmarks: A manual and trainer's guide*. Greensboro, NC:**
**   Center for Creative Leadership.**

Researchers at Recruit Co., Ltd., have successfully applied the CCL Key Events framework to understanding leadership in Japan. The same conclusion resulted as in the United States: leadership is developed through work experience.

Twenty-six next-generation leaders (high-potential middle managers) from nine companies were interviewed from July 2000 to June 2001. Interviewees were asked to describe three past work experiences that had made them develop dramatically, including what was learned through those experiences. The contents of the interviews were coded using CCL's framework.

Analyses of these data revealed a total of 206 events and lessons (average 7.9 per interviewee). Events and lessons similar to those found in the United States were also found in Japan. Some striking differences were found as well. The most frequently mentioned event among Japanese managers was the transition of switching from line to staff. According to Recruit Co., Ltd., this finding reflects the Japanese culture in which horizontal shifts are more acceptable. Other frequently mentioned events in Japan include early work experience and change in scope. A possible explanation for these differences may reside in the level of the Japanese managers, in that early work experiences may be more important for middle-level Japanese managers.

Another difference in the events was found with handling subordinate performance problems. No Japanese manager cited this type of event as an important teacher. The researchers hypothesized that it is more important in the United States for bosses to manage their direct reports than it is in Japan.

Six events unique to Japan were added. The events include managing several positions at the same time, tough superior/stretch management, customer dealings, serious discussions after 5 p.m., prior educational/ university experience, and observations/summary of the past.

Analyses of the lessons learned revealed developing task and managerial skills and managing divergent pressures to be the most frequently mentioned lessons (over 20 percent of the interviewees) in Japan. Five unique Japanese lessons were added: profound insights about the significance of work, understanding your role and fit within the organization, building teamwork and harmony, discovery and understanding of organizational culture, and designing change.

✳✳✳

Greathouse, C. L. (2001). Behavioral complexity as a mediator between leader characteristics and performance. *Dissertation Abstracts International: Section B. Sciences and Engineering, 61*(12-B), 6746.

Greathouse's dissertation uses CCL's 1994 to 1997 Leadership Development Program archival database of 2,000 managers to examine the antecedents and consequences of behavioral complexity, and how the relationship of behavioral complexity to performance changes as a function of managerial level, job function, and environment. Greathouse employed four instruments—the CCL Participant Background Form, the California Psychological Inventory (CPI), the Kirton Adaption-Innovation Inventory (KAI), and Benchmarks—to test 12 hypotheses using a variety of statistical techniques. Her results indicate that managers who are high on social perceptiveness (additive score from CPI empathy scale and Benchmarks self-awareness) and social adaptability (Benchmarks acting with flexibility and KAI) demonstrate the highest levels of behavioral complexity (averaged supervisor, peer, and direct report ratings for eight Benchmarks scales), which reduces derailment behaviors, which in turn enhances promotability. Social assertiveness (CPI dominance and independence scales) was found to hinder behavioral complexity, but it is hypothesized that this detrimental effect might be mitigated by high levels of social perceptiveness and social adaptability. Greathouse further found that the display of behavioral complexity is more important to the success of managers who work in complex versus routine environments as measured by promotability.

Greathouse's research emphasizes the importance of developing managers to effectively demonstrate all aspects of leadership (including adaptive, task, stability, and people) and to pay attention to the role the leader's environment can play in the developmental process.

✳✳✳

Leslie, J. B., & Schroeder, Q. (2001). The relationship between Benchmarks and MBTI. In *Benchmarks: A manual and trainer's guide*. Greensboro, NC: Center for Creative Leadership.

This study examined the relationship between scores on Benchmarks and a self-reported personality instrument, the Myers-Briggs Type Indicator (MBTI). The MBTI is one of the most widely used personality instruments with managers in leadership development efforts. Scores on the instrument reflect an individual's preferences on four bipolar dimensions: extraversion-introversion (E-I), sensing-intuition (S-I), thinking-feeling (T-F), and judging-perceiving (J-P). The E-I preference refers to an individual's attitudes or orientations toward life. In the extraverted attitude attention flows out, whereas in the introverted attitude energy is drawn in from the environment. The S-I preference refers to the ways that we become aware of things, people, events, or ideas, either by observation through our senses or perception by insight (intuition). The ways we come to conclusions about our observations defines the T-F preference. Thinking judgment employs logical connections, whereas feeling judgment is derived from subjective thinking, that is, weighing values and merits of issues. The J-P dimension characterizes orientations toward the world, the need to seek closure (judging) or the preference to remain open to events, information, and changes (perceiving). See Myers and McCaulley (1985) for more information on the MBTI.

Using a sample of 300 managers from CCL's Leadership Development Program, average Benchmarks ratings by coworkers (boss, peers, direct reports) were correlated with managers' MBTI scores. All the dimensions are associated with coworkers' perceptions. The thinking-feeling dimension is most associated with the Benchmarks scales. It appears that Benchmarks is measuring skills and perspectives that come naturally to feeling managers. Their inclination to rely on feeling-based judgments as opposed to thinking-based judgments seems to have led to strengths related to team building and relationship management.

Leadership scales that strongly relate ($r > .15$) to MBTI preferences include participative management, balance between personal life and work, and putting people at ease. More specifically, extraverted managers are perceived by their coworkers (bosses, peers, and direct reports) to be more participative in their management style than are introverted managers. In addition, managers rated significantly higher by their bosses on participative management have preferences for feeling and perceiving rather than thinking and judging. Likewise, managers who prefer feeling are seen by their bosses to have better balance between their work and personal life. Finally, managers with a preference for sensing over intuition received higher ratings by their bosses for putting people at ease.

$$* * *$$

Ruderman, M. N., Hannum, K., Leslie, J. B., & Steed, J. L. (2001). Leadership skills and emotional intelligence. In *Benchmarks: A manual and trainer's guide*. Greensboro, NC: Center for Creative Leadership.

Research comparing scores on Benchmarks to self-reported emotional intelligence scores revealed key Benchmarks leadership skills and perspectives and career flaws to be related to aspects of emotional intelligence. This research suggests that exploring emotional intelligence in general, and competencies such as stress tolerance, social responsibility, and impulse control in particular, may be additional ways managers can develop key Benchmarks leadership skills and perspectives. Over 300 managers attending CCL's Leadership Development Program between July and September 2000 volunteered to take part in this research by completing Benchmarks and the BarOn Emotional Quotient Inventory (BarOn EQ-i), which assesses components of emotional intelligence. The BarOn EQ-i has 15 scales that can be divided into five larger groupings. The areas assessed include emotional self-awareness, assertiveness, self-regard, self-actualization, independence, empathy, interpersonal relationships, social responsibility, problem solving, reality testing, flexibility, stress tolerance, impulse control, happiness, and optimism. The BarOn EQ-i was selected because it had the greatest body of scientific data, suggesting it was an accurate and reliable means of assessing emotional intelligence.

In the comparison of Benchmarks scores with BarOn EQ-i scores, 10 of the 16 skills and perspectives are moderately associated ($r = >.20$) with the emotional intelligence measures. Higher levels of emotional intelligence are associated with better performance in the following areas: participative management, putting people at ease, self-awareness, balance between personal life and work, straightforwardness and composure, building and mending relationships, doing whatever it takes, decisiveness, confronting problem employees, and change management.

Leadership abilities vary according to rater perspective and level of emotional intelligence. In general, coworkers seem to appreciate managers' abilities to control their impulses and anger, to withstand adverse events and stressful situations, to be happy with life, and to be a cooperative member of the group. These leaders are more likely to be seen as participative, self-aware, composed, and balanced.

In contrast, the absence of emotional intelligence was related to career derailment. Low emotional intelligence scores are related to problems with interpersonal relationships and having difficulty changing or adapting. Ratings on problems with interpersonal relationships from all coworkers—bosses, peers, and direct reports—were associated with low scores on impulse control. Problems with interpersonal relationships ratings from direct reports and peers were related to stress tolerance, and ratings from direct reports were related to social responsibility. These results suggest that managers who don't feel a responsibility to others, can't handle stress, are unaware of their own emotions, lack the ability to understand others, or erupt into anger easily are viewed as likely to derail because of problems dealing with other people. High scores on difficulty changing or adapting from direct reports were related to EQ-i scores on stress tolerance and impulse control. Resisting change and growth, as high scores on this derailment factor imply, may be plainly visible to direct reports.

❋ ❋ ❋

Brave, F. (2002). Learning for leadership. In *Benchmarks: A manual and trainer's guide*. Greensboro, NC: Center for Creative Leadership.

A replication of CCL's Key Events framework in the Netherlands confirmed CCL's findings that certain types of experiences produce learning. It also noted some differences. The study, conducted in 2001, is published in a book titled *Learning for Leadership: A New Vision on Management Development* (currently available only in Dutch).

For this study, 35 senior executives from five companies were interviewed about three key learning experiences. The researchers found that managers learn from events such as special assignments and setbacks, conflicting standards and values, role models, and interactions with those who work under them, similar to CCL's findings. In the Dutch study, however, more emphasis was placed on power and politics, as well as on personal events outside the workplace that contribute to development.

The Third Decade: 2003–2012

While the third decade is still open for Benchmarks publications, derailment seems to be a hot topic. The study of derailment is noted in eight annotations. These studies compared derailment potential to emotional intelligence; MBTI; self-other agreement among European, Asian, and Hispanic managers; college and university administrators; and finally, social exchange theory.

Other topics spiking in the literature include a comparison of leadership effectiveness to emotional intelligence, work-life balance, career advancement, role commitment, mentoring, and the effects of 9/11. Benchmarks continues to be recognized as a useful instrument in Buros Mental Measurements Yearbook (two annotations). Finally, self-other ratings continue to be a topic of study.

Bar, M. A., & Raju, N. S. (2003). IRT-based assessment of rater effects in multiple-source feedback instruments. *Organizational Research Methods*, *6*(1), 15–43.

Three item response theory (IRT)-based models of assessing measurement equivalence in 360-degree feedback were compared in this study. First, unidimensionality was tested because all three methods were based on IRT. Then, data from 491 managers, collected using the Benchmarks instrument, was analyzed in three ways: using traditional differential item functioning (DIF), Muraki's rater's effect (RE) model, and Patz, Junker, and Johnson's hierarchical rater model (HRM). Results indicate that the DIF assessment primarily provides information about the rater's conception of the ratee's ability. The RE and HRM frameworks provide a more accurate assessment of rater leniency/severity. Furthermore, even though rater source effects of leniency and severity were statistically significant, this was not observed at the item and scale levels.

✶✶✶

Carty, H. M. (2003). Review of Benchmarks (revised). In B. S. Plake, J. Impara, & R. A. Spies (Eds.), *The fifteenth mental measurements yearbook* **(pp. 123–124). Lincoln, NE: Buros Institute of Mental Measurements.**

The reviewer finds that, overall, the revised Benchmarks is a very useful multirater instrument which provides meaningful feedback about executive success. It is a helpful tool, based on sound research, for identifying strengths and developmental needs of managers. Some critiques in the first published review (Zedeck, 1995) of Benchmarks were the overrepresentation of white males and the underrepresentation of females during instrument construction. Although African Americans were added in the revised Benchmarks, more minorities and women need to be included. Other areas critiqued that remain unanswered in the revised version are the inclusiveness and generalizability of the norm group, the efficacy of the developmental process, and the future outcomes for the managers who participate in this process.

* * *

Douglas, C. A. (2003). *Key events and lessons for managers in a diverse workforce: A report on research and findings.* **Greensboro, NC: Center for Creative Leadership.**

This study replicates and extends the seminal work of McCall et al. (1988) on lessons and experiences that influence the development of managers. In particular, this study examines three questions: What are the significant events from which African American managers learn and develop? Are these significantly different from those of white managers? Are there new experiences or lessons learned since the 1980s?

The study included 160 white (121 male, 39 female) and 128 African American (81 male, 47 female) managers. The participants ranged in age from 28 to 59 with an average reported age of 44. The years of education ranged from 6 to 25, with an average of 17. Additionally, for both ethnicity samples, the gender means and standard deviations appear comparable.

Participants were asked to complete a survey that included the identification of three career-related events that made a difference in how they manage. In addition, they were asked to provide demographic information (race, gender, age, years of education, degrees awarded, organizational level, function, type of organization, number of employees, and compensation). Participants reported a total of 813 key events.

Initially, two CCL staff members, a white female and an African American male, coded the data. After randomly selecting 193 events for coding, both individuals independently coded the events. Once the events section was completed, the coders discussed discrepancies to reach agreement. The overall agreement between the two sets of events codes was .89. Within event categories, agreement ranged from .6 to 1.0. Next, after randomly selecting 147 lessons for coding, both individuals independently coded the lessons learned. Once the lessons section was completed, the coders discussed discrepancies to reach agreement. The overall agreement between the two raters for lessons was .79. Within lesson categories, agreement ranged from .69 to 1.0. Hence, interrater reliability was high overall for this study.

The event results suggest meaningful differences between the two ethnic groups. African American male managers experienced more hardships than their counterparts, whereas white male managers experienced more challenging assignments. Another finding was that mentors provided support in a difficult environment for African American male managers, whereas mentors were not found to be as influential to white male managers. Comparing experiences of female and male managers, females had more hardships, more supportive mentor findings, and less challenging assignments. Interestingly, these event findings mirror the African American manager findings.

The lesson results suggest that African American male managers reported learning from workplace racism and cynicism, whereas more white male managers reported learning from managing the work. Comparing lessons across gender, women reported learning more about themselves, such as increased self-awareness and learning from feedback, whereas males reported learning more lessons about the development of skills and knowledge to help them effectively manage the work.

✳ ✳ ✳

Lee, C. H., & Ang, S. (2003). *Assessing the measurement equivalence of Benchmarks between United States and Singapore* **(Technical Report). Singapore: Center for Cultural Intelligence; Division of Strategy, Management, & Organization; Nanyang Business School; Nanyang Technological University.**

Research comparing common conceptualizations of leadership effectiveness between Singapore and the United States was conducted using Benchmarks. The U.S. sample included 1,393 middle- to upper-level managers from CCL's Leadership Development Program. These data included self-, peer, supervisor, and subordinates ratings. Sixty percent of the sample was male, and the mean age of the U.S. group was 43. The Singapore sample of 1,393 (self, peer, supervisor, and subordinates) consisted of executives who attended training courses at the Nanyang Business School and participants who attended the Leadership Development Program conducted by CCL in Singapore. Seventy-nine percent of the Singapore sample was male, and the mean age was 34. Ninety-one percent of the Singapore sample was Chinese, 2 percent Malay, 3 percent Indian, 1 percent Eurasian, and 3 percent others (people from other ethnic backgrounds).

Hypotheses relating to the equivalence of Benchmarks measurement and structure across Singapore and U.S. executives were examined using a Confirmatory Factor Analysis, or CFA. In the first phase, the a priori measurement model comprising all the current Benchmarks items was tested in each country. Once an acceptable measurement model was identified for each country, the data from the two countries were combined and analyzed simultaneously. The proposed new model consisted of 63 items of 14 latent factors (the 4th and 14th factors in the a priori model, decisiveness and putting people at ease, were eliminated), which were nearly identical between the two countries.

Results of the selected fit indices (NFI, CFI, and GFI) were all well above .90, indicating that the baseline model provided an adequate fit to these data. The selected indices indicate that a common structure underlies all respondents' responses to the 63 items on Benchmarks between the two countries. Specifying the factor loadings to be equivalent across the two countries resulted in an insignificant difference in the χ^2 values for the baseline and invariant models, $\Delta\chi^2(51) = 7878.96, p > .10$. The 63 items on Benchmarks compose a multifaceted measure of leadership effectiveness that is equivalent across the two countries.

This research shows that the two countries share a common conceptualization of the leadership effectiveness dimensions underlying the reduced set of 63 Benchmarks items.

✳ ✳ ✳

Leslie, J. B. (2003). Gender differences in Benchmarks scores. In *Benchmarks: A manual and trainer's guide*. Greensboro, NC: Center for Creative Leadership.

An examination of mean differences on Benchmarks scores was conducted using a subsample of data collected from June 2000 through December 2002. Scores from 7,750 male managers and 3,973 female managers were examined using a One-Way ANOVA and Tukey's Studentized Range (HSD) Test to determine statistical significance difference. The results by rater group show that regardless of rater perspective, women tend to score higher on Benchmarks than men.

While rater group perspectives differ slightly, all raters, including the managers themselves, rated women managers higher or better on participative management, change management, compassion and sensitivity, self-awareness, putting people at ease, differences matter, and career management.

Differences by coworker groups are described as follows: Bosses rated female managers higher than males on resourcefulness, doing whatever it takes, straightforwardness and composure, decisiveness, leading employees, confronting problem employees, participative management, change management, building and mending relationships, compassion and sensitivity, self-awareness, putting people at ease, differences matter, and career management. Male managers were rated higher by their bosses on the derailment scales only (lower ratings are preferred).

Peers rated female managers higher than males on resourcefulness, doing whatever it takes, being a quick study, decisiveness, leading employees, confronting problem employees, participative management, change management, building and mending relationships, compassion and sensitivity, self-awareness, putting people at ease, differences matter, and career management. Male managers were rated higher by their peers on the derailment scales problems with interpersonal relationships, difficulty building and leading a team, difficulty changing or adapting, and failure to meet business objectives.

Direct reports rated female managers higher than males on resourcefulness, doing whatever it takes, being a quick study, decisiveness, leading employees, confronting problem employees, participative management, change management, building and mending relationships, straightforwardness and composure, self-awareness, putting people at ease, compassion and sensitivity, differences matter, and career management. Male managers were rated higher by direct reports on the derailment scales except for too narrow functional orientation.

Does this mean women are better managers and men are more likely to derail? These norm differences clearly suggest that female and male managers are perceived differently when it comes to Benchmarks skills and perspectives and derailment potential. The actual differences between mean scores, however, are less than half a point on a five-point scale. To answer questions about a practical meaningful difference, Cohen's (1988) effect size for means and standard deviations were calculated, and four scales— compassion and sensitivity, putting people at ease, differences matter, and career management—had small (approximately 15 percent) overlap but some practical meaningful difference.

✳ ✳ ✳

Leslie, J. B., & Balu, M. (2003). The relationship between Benchmarks and FIRO-B. In *Benchmarks: A manual and trainer's guide*. Greensboro, NC: Center for Creative Leadership.

This study examined the relationship between scores on Benchmarks and a self-reported personality assessment, Fundamental Interpersonal Relationship Orientation-Behavior (FIRO-B). FIRO-B is a commonly used personality instrument with managers in leadership development efforts. Feedback on the FIRO-B focuses the individual on interpersonal issues that may help or hinder effectiveness. FIRO-B measures three dimensions of interpersonal behavior: inclusion, control, and affection. Scores on the instrument range from 0 (behaviors are expressed or wanted very little) to 9 (frequent expression of or strong need for the characteristic behaviors).

Using a sample of 6,517 managers from CCL's Leadership Development Program, average Benchmarks scores were correlated with FIRO-B scores. Many of the leadership skills and perspectives are associated with FIRO-B interpersonal dimensions, though only a few were moderately associated ($r > .20$).

The leadership scales compassion and sensitivity, putting people at ease, and career management more strongly related to the FIRO-B dimensions expressed and wanted affection and expressed inclusion. More specifically, managers who are comfortable initiating social activity and whose interpersonal skills make meeting new people and sustaining social contacts easy and enjoyable are likely to put people at ease and manage their own careers. In addition, managers who are usually comfortable being warm and open with others (expressed affection) tend to rate themselves higher on putting people at ease and career management. Also, managers who are compassionate and sensitive to the needs of other people tend to rate higher on expressed and wanted affection.

Finally, managers in our sample who rate high on putting people at ease and career management tend to rate themselves high on expressed inclusion. These managers do not, however, rate themselves high on wanted inclusion.

✳ ✳ ✳

Ruderman, M. N., Hannum, K., Leslie, J. B., & Steed, J. L. (2003). Emotional intelligence and career derailment. *Competency & Emotional Intelligence*, *10*(3), 39–41.

This paper is similar to Ruderman, Hannum, Leslie, and Steed (2001).

***

Spangler, M. (2003). Review of Benchmarks (revised). In B. S. Plake, J. Impara, & R. A. Spies (Eds.), *The fifteenth mental measurements yearbook* (pp. 124–126). Lincoln, NE: Buros Institute of Mental Measurements.

This reviewer finds the description of the revised Benchmarks norming process to be comprehensive, and calls the sampling methods sound. Differential validity, content validity, and reliability are all well examined. However, this reviewer shares the concern of Sheldon Zedeck (1995) regarding influence on the future outcomes of the managers that participate in this developmental process. Nevertheless, the instrument is easy to administer and to understand, and the package that accompanies it is particularly helpful.

***

Bryson, K. D. (2005). Managerial success and derailment: The relationship between emotional intelligence and leadership. *Dissertation Abstracts International: Section B. Sciences and Engineering, 66*(1-B), 614.

Bryson's dissertation uses data from 103 CCL Leadership Development Program volunteer participants to examine the relationship between leadership skills as reported by a person and his or her raters and the emotional intelligence ability among managers. The volunteers completed Benchmarks and the Mayer-Salovey-Caruso Emotional Intelligence Test (MSCEIT), an ability measure of emotional intelligence instrument. Correlations between scores on the MSCEIT and Benchmarks leadership effectiveness, skills and perspectives, and derailment sections revealed a few weak relationships.

When correlations were found, leadership was associated with facilitating thought (the ability to use emotions to enhance the thought process) and managing emotions (the ability to be open to emotions and use them judiciously rather than acting without thinking), branches of emotional intelligence. Correlations between leadership and facilitating thought were predominately by the self-rater group. Leadership behaviors related to this emotional intelligence ability may include dealing with resistant employees, being open to input, not blaming others or situations for one's own mistakes, and managing others from different racial or cultural backgrounds. Derailment behaviors associated with this branch include being arrogant or bullying, and not encouraging or adapting.

Correlations between leadership and managing emotions were by the self-, boss, peer, and direct report rater groups. Some leadership behaviors related to this emotional intelligence ability include coaching, motivating, listening, finding common ground, and respecting and valuing diverse people. Derailment behaviors associated with this branch include resisting input, being dictatorial, adopting a bullying style, ordering people around, not motivating others, not adapting to different people, and not using feedback to make behavioral changes.

✳ ✳ ✳

Leslie, J. B., & Taylor, S. (2005). The negatives of focusing only on the positive. *Leadership in Action*, *24*(6), 17–18.

This study is based on information from the Benchmarks database collected between June 2000 and November 2004 from some 438,000 individuals: roughly 40,000 managers; 362,000 of their peers, direct reports, and other coworkers; and 36,000 of their direct bosses. More than 7,500 organizations, many of them Fortune 500 companies, are represented in the database. Using these data, CCL researchers have investigated several important underlying questions, including which leadership skills and perspectives managers' bosses consider to be critical for organizational success, and how strong coworkers consider managers to be in these critical skills and perspectives.

The bosses chose the following eight competencies most often: ability to lead employees (chosen by 89 percent of the bosses), resourcefulness (81 percent), decisiveness (75 percent), managing change (69 percent), straightforwardness and composure (68 percent), building and mending relationships (67 percent), doing whatever it takes (67 percent), and employing a participative management style (64 percent).

To determine workers' perceptions of managers' actual strengths, CCL researchers analyzed the ratings managers received from their peers, direct reports, and bosses on all 16 Benchmarks dimensions—nearly 400,000 ratings.

The findings were startling. The bosses' ranking of competencies most critical for organizational success was markedly different from the coworkers' ratings of managers' strengths. In fact, the competencies that bosses identified as most important for their organizations' success and presumably for the success of the managers in those organizations were in many cases not rated by coworkers as managerial strengths.

Thirteen of the 16 skills were rated below the statistical average for the database. That is, on the whole, the assessed managers were not considered strong in these 13 areas. Moreover, none of the eight skills that bosses rated as above average in importance received above average ratings as a managerial strength.

It's natural for managers to rely on their strengths until something in the leadership structure, the organization, or the environment changes and new skills may be required. Not everyone can be the best at all tasks, but people can learn, grow, and change. Strengths and talents can be developed, nurtured, and honed. However, the approach of focusing only on developing strengths not only limits human potential but may also restrict an organization's best performance to areas that are not the most important for the organization's future success.

∗ ∗ ∗

Gentry, W. A., Hannum, K. M., Ekelund, B. Z., & de Jong, A. (2007). A study of the discrepancy between self- and observer-ratings on managerial derailment characteristics of European managers. *European Journal of Work & Organizational Psychology, 16*(3), **295–325.**

This study was designed to determine whether discrepancies (that is, differences, dissimilarity, disagreement, incongruity) exist between self- and observer (subordinates, peers, and bosses) ratings about derailment. Results from 1,742 European managers revealed a statistically significant difference between managers' self-ratings and observer ratings on the extent to which a manager displayed derailment behaviors and characteristics. The results suggest an inflated self-observer discrepancy. Additionally, overestimators, or managers whose ratings were discrepant with observers, were those who were most likely to derail in the future. The discrepancy also widened as managerial level increased, and was mostly due to inflated self-ratings. In addition, an exploratory analysis showed that U.S. managers had a bigger self-observer rating discrepancy than European managers.

∗ ∗ ∗

Gentry, W. A., Mondore, S. P., & Cox, B. D. (2007). An exploratory study of managerial derailment characteristics and personality preferences. *Journal of Management Development, 26*, **857–873.**

This research was aimed at determining whether Myers-Briggs Type Indicator (MBTI) personality preferences and types were related to perceptions of managerial derailment. The sample comprised 6,124 managers whose mean age was 43 (range 26–66 years). Other demographic data revealed that 67 percent of the managers were male, 92 percent were Caucasian, and 45 percent had a bachelor's degree. Managers came from 1,889 different companies in 16 industries. Furthermore, 34 percent of the managers were top level, 47 percent were upper middle level, and 19 percent were middle level.

In general, the *t*-test results suggest small derailment differences between the different types: Intuitor managers were more prone to derailment tendencies than sensor managers. Similarly, thinker managers were more likely to show derailment tendencies than feeler managers. Finally, perceiver managers were more frequently seen as showing derailment tendencies than judging managers. With regard to type, sensing-feeling's (SFs) were rated as having the fewest derailment characteristics. In summary, there are distinct patterns between MBTI preferences and types of managers displaying derailment characteristics.

✳✳✳

Graves, L. M., Ohlott, P., & Ruderman, M. N. (2007). Commitment to family roles: Effects on managers' attitudes and performance. *Journal of Applied Psychology, 92*(1), 44–56.

Graves, Ohlott, and Ruderman investigated whether marital role commitment and parental role commitment have negative, positive, or simultaneously negative and positive effects on managers' life and career satisfaction, as well as on their performance. The work performance of 357 managers was measured using Benchmarks. The relationship between psychological strain and the effects of interference and enhancement on outcomes was also explored. Although the authors hypothesized that family role commitment would increase interference and thus reduce the favorability of outcomes, the results instead indicate that neither marital nor parental role commitment is associated with increased interference. Both marital role commitment and parental role commitment improved outcomes by increasing enhancement. In aggregate, marital and parental role commitment had more positive outcomes on work performance than negative.

✳✳✳

Gentry, W. A., Braddy, P. W., Fleenor, J. W., & Howard, P. J. (2008). Self-observer rating discrepancies on the derailment behaviors of Hispanic managers. *The Business Journal of Hispanic Research,* *2*(1), 76–87.

Research examining self-observer rating discrepancies for managers using measures of the negative aspects of leadership, such as managerial derailment, has been lacking. This study addresses this void in the literature by examining the effects of ethnicity on self-observer rating discrepancies in ratings of managerial derailment. Self-observer rating discrepancies were investigated on a measure of the characteristics and behaviors of managerial derailment of Hispanic managers as compared to managers of other ethnic groups (whites, blacks, and Asians). Data were collected from 1,362 managers using Benchmarks. Results from MANOVAs revealed that there were no statistically significant differences in the four rater groups' derailment ratings when comparing Hispanics and whites. Contrary to the results of previous research, self-observer rating discrepancies of derailment behaviors were comparable for Hispanics and whites. All three of these self-observer rating discrepancies were larger for blacks than for Hispanics. Also, these self-observer rating discrepancies were larger for Hispanics than for Asians.

✳✳✳

Gentry, W. A., & Shanock, L. R. (2008). Views of managerial derailment from above and below: The importance of a good relationship with upper management and putting people at ease. *Journal of Applied Social Psychology, 38,* 2469–2494.

A social exchange theory approach is taken to examine managerial behavior and whether positive treatment will trickle down from upper management through managers to lower-level employees. Data was collected from 1,978 managers using the Benchmarks instrument. Specifically, this study focuses on whether a manager's good relationship with upper management will lead the manager to put lower-level employees at ease. Putting others at ease is one characteristic of effective interpersonal relationships, which is an important indicator of not derailing. These hypotheses were supported, as well as the supposition that managers who put others at ease are also less likely to be perceived by their bosses, direct reports, and themselves as possessing characteristics of potential derailment.

✳✳✳

Gentry, W. A., Weber, T. J., & Sadri, G. (2008). Examining career-related mentoring and managerial performance across cultures: A multi-level analysis. *Journal of Vocational Behavior, 72,* 241–253.

Gentry, Weber, and Sadri extend mentoring research by examining career-related mentoring and how societal culture is related to the mentoring relationship. The researchers used Benchmarks and Project GLOBE (measuring the societal culture dimension of performance orientation) to gather data from a large international sample of over 30,000 managers from 33 countries in over 4,000 companies. Results supported hypotheses that how direct reports rate their managers on career-related mentoring behaviors is positively related to how bosses rate the managers on performance, and that performance orientation is a cross-level moderator.

✳✳✳

Lance, C. E., Hoffman, B. J., Gentry, W. A., & Baranik, L. E. (2008). Rater source factors represent important subcomponents of the criterion construct space, not rater bias. *Human Resource Management Review, 18,* 223–232.

Research on multisource performance ratings (MSPRs) such as Benchmarks has resulted in conflicting interpretations of the same evidence. Although within-source ratings show some convergence, there is low to moderate convergence in across-source ratings. While some view this low across-source convergence as a valuable insight into ratee performance, others view it as a source of rater bias. The authors of this review attempt to resolve these conflicting interpretations, suggesting that the difference may be the result of a possible improper application of multitrait-multimethod (MTMM) methodology to study MSPRs. They conclude that 360-degree feedback instruments offer multiple valuable, nonredundant perspectives of ratee performance, and they urge researchers to take a broader perspective on multifaceted measurement designs.

✳✳✳

Lyness, K. S., & Judiesch, M. K. (2008). Can a manager have a life and career? International and multisource perspectives on work-life balance and career advancement potential. *Journal of Applied Psychology, 93*(4), 789–805.

In this cross-national investigation about the relationship between managerial work-life balance and career advancement, researchers investigated whether managers perceived to be more work focused would be promoted more than work-life-balanced managers. Using Benchmarks, self-rating, peer-rating, and supervisor-rating data were collected from 9,627 managers in 33 countries. Results from multilevel analyses suggest that managers who were rated higher in work-life balance were also rated higher in career advancement potential. Their findings also support the use of multisource measures rather than simply relying on self-reports.

***

Sparks, T. E., & Gentry, W. A. (2008). Leadership competencies: An exploratory study of what is important now and what has changed since the terrorist attacks of 9/11. *Journal of Leadership Studies, 2(2), 22–35.*

This study explores and identifies the leadership competencies that managers believe are needed to be successful across different managerial levels and organization types, whether these competencies have remained the same over time, and whether the importance of certain leadership competencies change after traumatic events such as the 9/11 attacks in the United States. Results suggest that the leadership competencies leading employees and resourcefulness were the most important across managerial levels and organization types studied. Results also suggest that leadership competencies remain constant over time, even after such events as 9/11.

***

Atwater, L., Wang, M., Smither, J. W., & Fleenor, J. W. (2009). Are cultural characteristics associated with the relationship between self and others' ratings of leadership? *Journal of Applied Psychology, 94, 876–886.*

In this paper, Atwater, Wang, Smither, and Fleenor examine the relationship between self- and subordinate ratings of leadership and the relationship between self- and peer ratings of leadership for managers from 21 countries. The authors use a framework which suggests that environmental/sociocultural context influences behavioral and interpersonal characteristics, which in turn influences individual outcomes. They predicted that cultural context would influence the nature of verbal and nonverbal communication, which would affect the clarity, candor, and accuracy of interpersonal feedback and the relationship between leaders' self-ratings and ratings from their followers and peers. Benchmarks data from 964 managers in 21 countries were included in analyses. The measure of cultural practice—that is, individualism/ collectivism, assertiveness, and power distance—was taken from the GLOBE data collected and compiled on 62 countries.

Using multilevel modeling analyses, the authors found the main effects of individualism were significantly and positively related to leadership ratings from all three rating sources (for self-ratings, $\gamma_{02} = 0.107$, $z = 2.18$, $p < .05$; for peer ratings, $\gamma_{02} = 0.102$, $z = 1.85$, $p < .10$; for subordinate ratings, $\gamma_{02} = 0.107$, $z = 2.06$, $p < .05$), suggesting that leaders are more likely to give themselves higher ratings and to receive higher ratings from their peers and subordinates in cultures that are higher on individualism.

Further analyses revealed that the relationship between self- and peer ratings is stronger in cultures that are higher on assertiveness and the relationship between self- and subordinate ratings is stronger in cultures that are higher on assertiveness. Power distance was found to be significantly and positively related to the peer rating–self-rating slope ($\gamma_{13} = 0.119$, $z = 2.29$, $p < .05$). The relationship between self- and peer ratings was found to be stronger in cultures that have higher power distance. Power distance was also significantly related to the subordinate rating–self-rating slope but in the opposite direction from that hypothesized, suggesting that the relationship between self- and subordinate ratings is stronger in cultures that have higher power distance. Individualism did not show positive effects in predicting either the peer rating–self-rating slope or the subordinate rating–self-rating slope. Overall, this study found that cultural variables are related to the relationships between self- and other ratings. Results reveal the need for further cross-cultural research examining self-awareness and its relationship to managerial effectiveness.

✳ ✳ ✳

Gentry, W. A., Katz, R. B., & McFeeters, B. B. (2009). The continual need for improvement to avoid derailment: A study of college and university administrators. *Higher Education Research and Development*, *28*(3), 335–348.

Gentry, Katz, and McFeeters extend the derailment literature by examining whether willingness to improve is related to derailment in college and university administrators. Data from 173 participants in 88 U.S. colleges and universities were collected using Benchmarks, a multisource instrument that, among other constructs, measures both indicators of willingness to improve and derailment. Results indicate that the higher participants' self-reported willingness to improve was, the less likely their bosses were to report displays of derailment behaviors and characteristics. The reverse was true as well. Although self-observer discrepancies are common in multisource instruments, results also indicate that the more the participants' peers and direct reports believed that the participants were willing to improve, the less likely their bosses were to report displays of derailment indicators.

* * *

Stokely, D. R. (2009). A correlational study of emotional intelligence and successful leadership. *Dissertation Abstracts International: Section A. Humanities and Social Sciences, 69*(8-A), 3223.

Stokely's dissertation investigated the relationship between four variables of emotional intelligence and three variables of successful leadership among corporate executive leadership within the retail industry. Two instruments used in this explanatory correlational research were the Mayer-Salovey-Caruso Emotional Intelligence Test (MSCEIT) and Benchmarks. Stokely's findings revealed a correlation between emotional intelligence and successful leadership in the retail industry. Recommendations for further research include expanding future studies to encompass various retail subcategories to gain a perspective of the retail industry as a whole (that is, financial services, restaurants, auto dealerships, and convenience stores, among other retail businesses).

* * *

Eckert, R., Ekelund, B. Z., Gentry, W. A., & Dawson, J. F. (2010). "I don't see me like you see me, but is that a problem?" Cultural influences on rating discrepancy in 360-degree feedback instruments. *European Journal of Work and Organizational Psychology, 19*, 259–278.

Discrepancy between self- and observer ratings is common in 360-degree feedback from a variety of rater sources. It is frequently considered an indicator of problems in leadership, relationships, or skills, or simply a lack of self-awareness. Recently, there is more evidence to suggest that there are also systemic and contextual influences, such as cultural values, at play. This study investigates such antecedent influences on three leadership skills: decisiveness, leading employees, and managerial composure. The researchers hypothesized that in high-power distance cultures, higher self-observer rating discrepancies would be found in these leadership skills. The results partially supported the high-power distance effect on decisiveness, did not support its effect on leading employees, and did support its effect on managerial composure. The overall results strongly suggest that systemic and contextual influences such as cultural values do have an effect on self-observer rating discrepancies and should be taken into consideration when interpreting them.

$$* * *$$

Gentry, W. A., & Sosik, J. J. (2010). Developmental relationships and managerial promotability in organizations: A multisource study. *Journal of Vocational Behavior, 77*, 266–278.

From both leadership and mentoring research, the literature suggests that mentoring benefits direct reports. This study extends both leadership and mentoring literature by investigating whether the benefits are bidirectional, that is, whether mentoring managers also receive a benefit. To this end, Gentry and Sosik examined whether mentoring behaviors from a manager to his or her direct reports led to higher perceptions of that manager's promotability.

For this study, a multisource sample comprising 1,623 managers from 250 companies was used. Of this sample, the mean age was 45, 65 percent were male, 88 percent were white, 87 percent had received at least a bachelor's degree, and they averaged 4.5 years in their current position. This sample was derived from participants of organizations that had purchased and completed the Benchmarks questionnaire.

To examine the relationship between mentoring and the perception of promotability, two measures were used. To measure mentoring, Gentry and Sosik used six items from Benchmarks. Since items were derived from a previous study, the authors conducted confirmatory analyses and found that Cronbach's alpha = .79 for self-ratings and .91 for direct report ratings. To assess promotability, the authors used three research items and averaged three items ($\alpha = .89$) to measure promotability from at least one boss and one peer. Both measures were found to be statistically justifiable for measuring the constructs, mentoring and promotability.

Results show that after controlling for demographic variables such as gender, level of management, age, ethnicity, and education, self-ratings of career-related mentoring was positively associated with both boss and peer ratings of promotability perceptions, and accounted for a statistically significant amount of the variance ($\Delta R^2 = .01, p < .01$), respectively. Further, direct report ratings of career-related mentoring was also positively associated with both boss and peer ratings of promotability perceptions, and accounted for a statistically significant amount of the variance ($\Delta R^2 = .04$, $p < .01$) and ($\Delta R^2 = .07$, $p < .01$), respectively. Hence, the findings suggest that career-related mentoring is positively associated with promotability perception. Moreover, within a self-other rating framework using polynomial regression and response surface analysis, (a) higher ratings of career-related mentoring by focal managers and their direct reports were positively related to both boss and peer ratings of focal managers' promotability, and (b) underraters (those with self-ratings of mentoring behaviors that were lower than direct report ratings) had higher promotability ratings from bosses and peers than did overraters (those with self-ratings of mentoring behaviors that were higher than direct report ratings).

✳ ✳ ✳

Gentry, W. A., Yip, J., & Hannum, K. M. (2010). Self-observer rating discrepancies of managers in Asia: A study of derailment characteristics and behaviors in Southern and Confucian Asia. *International Journal of Selection and Assessment, 18,* 237–250.

Multisource ratings were investigated in this study of 860 Asian managers from the regions of Southern Asia ($n = 261$) and Confucian Asia ($n = 599$). The authors analyzed cultural differences in self-observer rating discrepancies using multivariate regression procedures. The findings revealed that the self-observer rating discrepancy was wider for managers from Southern Asia as compared to Confucian Asia. The discrepancy was driven by managers' different self-ratings across cultures rather than by observer ratings from managers' bosses, direct reports, or peers. Cultural differences in self- and observer ratings within Asia also provide implications for the practice of multisource assessments within that part of the world.

✳ ✳ ✳

Hoffman, B. J., Lance, C. E., Bynum, B. H., & Gentry, W. A. (2010). Rater source effects are alive and well after all. *Personnel Psychology, 63,* 119–151.

In response to recent research that questions the importance of rater source effects on multisource performance ratings (MSPRs) such as Benchmarks, this study reexamines the impact of rater source on MSPRs through the use of hierarchical confirmatory factor analysis. The results indicate that source effects explain more variance in MSPRs and support the value of collecting performance data from multiple sources (that is, boss, peers, and direct reports) at different organizational levels.

References

Atwater, L., Ostroff, C., Yammarino, F., & Fleenor, J. (1998). Self-other agreement: Does it matter? *Personnel Psychology, 51*, 577–598.

Atwater, L., Wang, M., Smither, J. W., & Fleenor, J. W. (2009). Are cultural characteristics associated with the relationship between self and others' ratings of leadership? *Journal of Applied Psychology, 94*, 876–886.

Bar, M. A., & Raju, N. S. (2003). IRT-based assessment of rater effects in multiple-source feedback instruments. *Organizational Research Methods, 6*(1), 15–43.

Bar-On, R. (1999). *BarOn emotional quotient inventory: A measure of emotional intelligence: Technical manual*. Toronto, Canada: Multi-Health Systems.

Brave, F. (2002). Learning for leadership. In *Benchmarks: A manual and trainer's guide*. Greensboro, NC: Center for Creative Leadership.

Brutus, S., Fleenor, J. W., & London, M. (1998). Does 360-degree feedback work in different industries? A between-industry comparison of the reliability and validity of multi-source performance ratings. *Journal of Management Development, 17*(5), 177–190.

Brutus, S., Fleenor, J. W., & McCauley, C. D. (1999). Demographic and personality predictors of congruence in multi-source ratings. *Journal of Management Development, 18*(5), 417–435.

Brutus, S., London, M., & Martineau, J. (1999). The impact of 360-degree feedback on planning for career development. *Journal of Management Development, 18*(8), 676–693.

Bryson, K. D. (2005). Managerial success and derailment: The relationship between emotional intelligence and leadership. *Dissertation Abstracts International: Section B. Sciences and Engineering, 66*(1-B), 614.

Carty, H. M. (2003). Review of Benchmarks (revised). In B. S. Plake, J. Impara, & R. A. Spies (Eds.), *The fifteenth mental measurements yearbook* (pp. 123–124). Lincoln, NE: Buros Institute of Mental Measurements.

Center for Creative Leadership. (1997). CPI/MBTI/Benchmarks study. In *Benchmarks: A manual and trainer's guide*. Greensboro, NC: Center for Creative Leadership.

Center for Creative Leadership. (1997). Gender differences: Updates on Key Events research for women of the 90's. In *Benchmarks: A manual and trainer's guide*. Greensboro, NC: Center for Creative Leadership.

Center for Creative Leadership. (1997). Gender differences: Validity study. In *Benchmarks: A manual and trainer's guide*. Greensboro, NC: Center for Creative Leadership.

Center for Creative Leadership. (1997). Organizational cultural differences. In *Benchmarks: A manual and trainer's guide*. Greensboro, NC: Center for Creative Leadership.

Center for Creative Leadership. (1997). Race differences: Are African-American managers rated differently than white managers? In *Benchmarks: A manual and trainer's guide*. Greensboro, NC: Center for Creative Leadership.

Center for Creative Leadership. (1997). Relationships with other psychological instruments. In *Benchmarks: A manual and trainer's guide*. Greensboro, NC: Center for Creative Leadership.

Center for Creative Leadership. (2001). Japanese key events. In *Benchmarks: A manual and trainer's guide*. Greensboro, NC: Center for Creative Leadership.

Cohen, J. (1988). *Statistical power analysis for the behavioral sciences* (2nd ed.). Hillsdale, NJ: Lawrence Erlbaum Associates.

Conway, J. M. (2000). Managerial performance development constructs and personality correlates. *Human Performance*, *13*(1), 23–46.

Conway, R. L. (2000). The impact of coaching mid-level managers utilizing multi-rater feedback. *Dissertation Abstracts International: Section A. Humanities and Social Sciences*, *60*(7-A), 2672.

Douglas, C. A. (2003). *Key events and lessons for managers in a diverse work-force: A report on research and findings*. Greensboro, NC: Center for Creative Leadership.

Eckert, R., Ekelund, B. Z., Gentry, W. A., & Dawson, J. F. (2010). "I don't see me like you see me, but is that a problem?" Cultural influences on rating discrepancy in 360-degree feedback instruments. *European Journal of Work and Organizational Psychology*, *19*, 259–278.

Fleenor, J. (1997). The relationship between the MBTI and measures of personality and performance in management groups. In C. Fitzgerald & L. K. Kirby (Eds.), *Developing leaders: Research and applications in psychological type and leadership development* (pp. 115–138). Palo Alto, CA: Davies-Black.

Fleenor, J. W., McCauley, C. D., & Brutus, S. (1996). Self-other rating agreement and leader effectiveness. *Leadership Quarterly*, *7*, 487–506.

Gentry, W. A., Braddy, P. W., Fleenor, J. W., & Howard, P. J. (2008). Self-observer rating discrepancies on the derailment behaviors of Hispanic managers. *The Business Journal of Hispanic Research*, *2*(1), 76–87.

Gentry, W. A., Hannum, K. M., Ekelund, B. Z., & de Jong, A. (2007). A study of the discrepancy between self- and observer-ratings on managerial derailment characteristics of European managers. *European Journal of Work & Organizational Psychology, 16*(3), 295–325.

Gentry, W. A., Katz, R. B., & McFeeters, B. B. (2009). The continual need for improvement to avoid derailment: A study of college and university administrators. *Higher Education Research and Development, 28*(3), 335–348.

Gentry, W. A., Mondore, S. P., & Cox, B. D. (2007). An exploratory study of managerial derailment characteristics and personality preferences. *Journal of Management Development, 26*, 857–873.

Gentry, W. A., & Shanock, L. R. (2008). Views of managerial derailment from above and below: The importance of a good relationship with upper management and putting people at ease. *Journal of Applied Social Psychology, 38*, 2469–2494.

Gentry, W. A., & Sosik, J. J. (2010). Developmental relationships and managerial promotability in organizations: A multisource study. *Journal of Vocational Behavior, 77*, 266–278.

Gentry, W. A., Weber, T. J., & Sadri, G. (2008). Examining career-related mentoring and managerial performance across cultures: A multilevel analysis. *Journal of Vocational Behavior, 72*, 241–253.

Gentry, W. A., Yip, J., & Hannum, K. M. (2010). Self-observer rating discrepancies of managers in Asia: A study of derailment characteristics and behaviors in Southern and Confucian Asia. *International Journal of Selection and Assessment, 18*, 237–250.

Graves, L. M., Ohlott, P., & Ruderman, M. N. (2007). Commitment to family roles: Effects on managers' attitudes and performance. *Journal of Applied Psychology, 92*(1), 44–56.

Greathouse, C. L. (2001). Behavioral complexity as a mediator between leader characteristics and performance. *Dissertation Abstracts International: Section B. Sciences and Engineering, 61*(12-B), 6746.

Greguras, G. J., & Robie, C. (1998). A new look at within-source interrater reliability of 360-degree feedback ratings. *Journal of Applied Psychology, 83*(6), 960–968.

Hoffman, B. J., Lance, C. E., Bynum, B. H., & Gentry, W. A. (2010). Rater source effects are alive and well after all. *Personnel Psychology, 63*, 119–151.

Hood, S. J. (1996). A study of self and direct report perceptions of the skills and performance competencies important for superintendent effectiveness. *Dissertation Abstracts International: Section A. Humanities and Social Sciences, 57*(5-A), 1928.

Lance, C. E., Hoffman, B. J., Gentry, W. A., & Baranik, L. E. (2008). Rater source factors represent important subcomponents of the criterion construct space, not rater bias. *Human Resource Management Review, 18*, 223–232.

Lee, C. H., & Ang, S. (2003). *Assessing the measurement equivalence of Benchmarks between United States and Singapore* (Technical Report). Singapore: Center for Cultural Intelligence; Division of Strategy, Management, & Organization; Nanyang Business School; Nanyang Technological University.

Leslie, J. B. (2003). Gender differences in Benchmarks scores. In *Benchmarks: A manual and trainer's guide*. Greensboro, NC: Center for Creative Leadership.

Leslie, J. B., & Balu, M. (2003). The relationship between Benchmarks and FIRO-B. In *Benchmarks: A manual and trainer's guide*. Greensboro, NC: Center for Creative Leadership.

Leslie, J. B., & Schroeder, Q. (2001). The relationship between Benchmarks and MBTI. In *Benchmarks: A manual and trainer's guide*. Greensboro, NC: Center for Creative Leadership.

Leslie, J. B., & Taylor, S. (2005). The negatives of focusing only on the positive. *Leadership in Action, 24*(6), 17–18.

Leslie, J. B., & Van Velsor, E. (1996). *A look at derailment today: North America and Europe* (Report No. 169). Greensboro, NC: Center for Creative Leadership.

Lindsey, E., Homes, V., & McCall, M. W., Jr. (1987). *Key events in executives' lives* (Report No. 32). Greensboro, NC: Center for Creative Leadership.

Lombardo, M., & McCauley, C. (1988). *The dynamics of management derailment*. Greensboro, NC: Center for Creative Leadership.

Lombardo, M., Ruderman, M., & McCauley, C. (1988). Explanations of success and derailment in upper-level management positions. *Journal of Business and Psychology, 2*, 199–216.

Lyness, K. S., & Judiesch, M. K. (2008). Can a manager have a life and career? International and multisource perspectives on work-life balance and career advancement potential. *Journal of Applied Psychology, 93*(4), 789–805.

McCall, M. W., Jr., & Lombardo, M. M. (1983). *Off the track: Why and how successful executives get derailed*. Greensboro, NC: Center for Creative Leadership.

McCall, M. W., Jr., & Lombardo, M. M. (1983, February). What makes a top executive? *Psychology Today, 17*(2), 26–31.

McCall, M. W., Jr., Lombardo, M. M., & Morrison, A. M. (1988). *The lessons of experience: How successful executives develop on the job*. Lexington, MA: Lexington Books.

McCauley, C. D., & Lombardo, M. M. (1990). Benchmarks: An instrument for diagnosing managerial strengths and weaknesses. In K. Clark & M. Clark (Eds.), *Measures of leadership* (pp. 535–545). West Orange, NJ: Leadership Library of America.

McCauley, C. D., Lombardo, M. M., & Usher, C. J. (1989). Diagnosing management development needs: An instrument based on how managers develop. *Journal of Management, 15*, 389–403.

Morrison, A. M., White, R. P., & Van Velsor, E. (1987). *Breaking the glass ceiling: Can women reach the top of America's largest corporations?* Reading, MA: Addison-Wesley.

Myers, I. B., & McCaulley, M. H. (1985). *Manual: A guide to the development and use of the Myers-Briggs Type Indicator*. Palo Alto, CA: Consulting Psychologists Press.

Raju, N. S., Leslie, J. B., McDonald-Mann, D., & Craig, B. (1999). Content validation. In *Benchmarks: A manual and trainer's guide*. Greensboro, NC: Center for Creative Leadership.

Ruderman, M. N., Hannum, K., Leslie, J. B., & Steed, J. L. (2001). Leadership skills and emotional intelligence. In *Benchmarks: A manual and trainer's guide*. Greensboro, NC: Center for Creative Leadership.

Ruderman, M. N., Hannum, K., Leslie, J. B., & Steed, J. L. (2003). Emotional intelligence and career derailment. *Competency & Emotional Intelligence, 10*(3), 39–41.

Spangler, M. (2003). Review of Benchmarks (revised). In B. S. Plake, J. Impara, & R. A. Spies (Eds.), *The fifteenth mental measurements yearbook* (pp. 124–126). Lincoln, NE: Buros Institute of Mental Measurements.

Sparks, T. E., & Gentry, W. A. (2008). Leadership competencies: An exploratory study of what is important now and what has changed since the terrorist attacks of 9/11. *Journal of Leadership Studies, 2*(2), 22–35.

Stokely, D. R. (2009). A correlational study of emotional intelligence and successful leadership. *Dissertation Abstracts International: Section A. Humanities and Social Sciences, 69*(8-A), 3223.

Van Velsor, E., & Fleenor, J. (1997). The MBTI and leadership skills: Relationships between the MBTI and four 360-degree management feedback instruments. In C. Fitzgerald & L. K. Kirby (Eds.), *Developing leaders: Research and applications in psychological type and leadership development* (pp. 139–162). Palo Alto, CA: Davies-Black.

Van Velsor, E., & Hughes, M. (1990). *Gender differences in the development of managers: How women managers learn from experience.* Greensboro, NC: Center for Creative Leadership.

Van Velsor, E., & Leslie, J. B. (1995). Why executives derail: Perspectives across time and cultures. *Academy of Management Executive, 9*(4) 62–72.

Van Velsor, E., Taylor, S., & Leslie, J. B. (1993). An examination of the relationships among self-perception accuracy, self-awareness, gender, and leader effectiveness. *Human Resource Management, 32*(2-3), 249–263.

Wise, P. G. (1997). Rating differences in multi-rater feedback: A new look at an old issue. *Dissertation Abstracts International: Section B. Sciences and Engineering, 58*(6-B), 3352.

Zedeck, S. (1995). Review of Benchmarks. In J. Conoley & J. Impara (Eds.), *The twelfth mental measurements yearbook* (Vol. 1, pp. 128–129). Lincoln, NE: Buros Institute of Mental Measurements.

Appendix A: Research Organized by Primary Content

Category	First Author	Date	Page
Cultural	Van Velsor	1995	14
	Leslie	1996	17
	CCL	1997	20
	Raju	1999	29
	CCL	2001	32
	Brave	2002	36
	Lee	2003	39
	Gentry	2007	45
	Graves	2007	46
	Gentry	2008	47
	Gentry (2)	2008	47
	Lyness	2008	48
	Sparks	2008	49
	Atwater	2009	49
	Eckert	2010	51
	Gentry	2010	52
Derailment	McCall	1983	3
	McCall (2)	1983	4
	Morrison	1987	6
	Lombardo	1988	7
	Lombardo (2)	1988	8
	Van Velsor	1995	14
	Leslie	1996	17
	Ruderman	2003	42
	Bryson	2005	43
	Gentry	2007	45
	Gentry (2)	2007	45
	Gentry	2008	47
	Gentry (2)	2008	47
	Gentry	2009	50
	Gentry	2010	53
Emotional Intelligence	Ruderman	2001	35
	Ruderman	2003	42
	Bryson	2005	43
	Stokely	2009	51

Appendix A: **Research Organized by Primary Content** (continued)

Category	First Author	Date	Page
Ethnicity	CCL	1997	21
	Brutus	1999	27
	Raju	1999	29
	Douglas	2003	38
	Gentry	2008	47
Gender	Morrison	1987	6
	Van Velsor	1990	11
	Van Velsor	1993	13
	CCL	1997	19
	CCL (2)	1997	20
	Brutus	1999	27
	Leslie	2003	40
Key Events/	Lindsey	1987	5
Lessons of Experience	Morrison	1987	6
	McCall	1988	8
	Van Velsor	1990	11
	CCL	1997	19
	CCL	2001	32
	Brave	2002	36
	Douglas	2003	38
Mentoring/Coaching	Conway	2000	30
	Gentry	2008	48
	Gentry	2010	52
Personality	CCL	1997	17
	CCL	1997	22
	Fleenor	1997	23
	Van Velsor	1997	24
	Brutus	1999	27
	Conway	2000	30
	Greathouse	2001	33
	Leslie	2001	34
	Leslie	2003	42
	Gentry	2007	45

Appendix A: Research Organized by Primary Content (continued)

Category	First Author	Date	Page
Psychometrics	McCauley	1989	9
	McCauley	1990	10
	Zedeck	1995	15
	CCL	1997	21
	Brutus	1998	26
	Greguras	1998	27
	Raju	1999	29
	Bar	2003	37
	Carty	2003	37
	Lee	2003	39
	Spangler	2003	43
	Leslie	2005	44
Rating Differences/	Van Velsor	1993	13
360-Degree Feedback	Fleenor	1996	15
	Hood	1996	16
	Wise	1997	24
	Atwater	1998	25
	Brutus	1999	27
	Brutus (2)	1999	28
	Raju	1999	29
	Conway	2000	31
	Bar	2003	37
	Gentry	2007	45
	Gentry	2008	47
	Lance	2008	48
	Atwater	2009	49
	Hoffman	2010	53
	Eckert	2010	51
	Gentry	2010	53

Appendix B: Guidelines for Obtaining Access to CCL Databases

The Center for Creative Leadership (CCL®) maintains a number of databases on individuals who have participated in our programs or who have used our products, and we encourage researchers to use these data for research. The following guidelines are designed to aid researchers while providing the confidentiality we have guaranteed our clients *and* ensuring our own awareness and approval of all research being conducted with our data. The protection of CCL's reputation (and thus part of the value of using our data) depends on the integrity of our standards and processes.

These guidelines apply to researchers who are either working outside of CCL or in organizations affiliated with CCL, as well as to CCL employees or interns working on a project that is not CCL's. In all cases, researchers interested in obtaining access to any CCL program or product database should submit a proposal to CCL that outlines the following:

- The purpose and merits of the research
- What data are being requested, including
  - type of data (e.g., MBTI, Benchmarks), specifying relevant sections of each instrument for which data are requested (if applicable), and
  - characteristics of the desired sample (e.g., age of the data, sample size, demographics)
- How the data will be used, including the variables of interest and your proposed type of analysis
- The names and titles of all those who will have access to the data, whether or not they are working with it directly
- The credentials of the researcher(s) (including degree, institution, current affiliation, any relevant publications)
- A statement indicating you agree to the below expectations for acceptance
- Contact information for the primary researcher (address, phone, and e-mail)
- If you are a student, add a letter of support from your academic advisor, including his or her phone and e-mail.

- If you are interested in having CCL faculty collaborate with you on this project, please indicate so in your cover note. (We will let you know if there is someone whose research interests align with your proposed study.)

For a research project to be approved, it must have technical merit, be of interest to CCL, and be conceptually and methodologically sound. If your proposal is accepted, you are expected to do the following:

- Acknowledge CCL as your data source in the text of all papers resulting from research using CCL data. For example, "The author would like to thank the Center for Creative Leadership for providing the data used in this research."

- Use appropriate trademarks, service marks, and copyrights.

- Ensure that only researchers with CCL approval have access to these data. Data should not be shared (in electronic or printed format) with researchers who do not have CCL's prior consent, nor stored anywhere (e.g., on a server) that allows others to access it without permission. If it becomes necessary to include someone new in the research, contact CCL's Knowledge Management Director.

- Give CCL the opportunity to review any publications or presentations resulting from this research before they are submitted for publication: contact the Knowledge Management Director to determine if such a review is required.

- Provide CCL with a copy of any papers resulting from the research upon completion of the project. This includes, but is not limited to, dissertations, journal articles, book chapters, conference papers, and papers not published in a traditional format. *Even if a paper is rejected for publication, a copy must be provided to CCL.*

- Delete the raw data one year after the research is complete. Exceptions to this requirement may be requested—contact the Knowledge Management Director.

- If you decide to do an additional study with the same dataset, submit another proposal for approval.

We strongly encourage sample heterogeneity whenever feasible to enhance the relevance and applicability of the proposed research to diverse populations. Any data made available for research will be stripped of information that could lead to the identification of individual participants or their organizations. Approval decisions are made on a case-by-case basis.

For more information contact Client Services at +1 336 545 2810.

Ordering Information

To get more information, to order other CCL Press publications, or to find out about bulk-order discounts, please contact us by phone at +1 336 545 2810 or visit our online bookstore at **www.ccl.org/publications**.

LaVergne, TN USA
23 March 2011
221290LV00002B/86/P

9 781604 910858